Growing Up
In Amityville:
In Their Own Words

Stories about growing up

on Long Island's south shore

in the 1950s, '60s and '70s.

Edited by Doug Robinson

Printed in the United States of America

First Printing: September 2021

Lulu.com

978-1-105-70785-8

Imprint: Lulu.com

INTRODUCTION

Amityville, N.Y., sits on the south shore of Long Island about 40 miles east of New York City. It was settled in the late 1600s by English immigrants moving west from Massachusetts, south across the Long Island Sound, then south across Long Island. They came for the bounty of the Great South Bay; salt hay, fish, clams and oysters.

During and after WWII there was a second significant migration of people from the New York City metropolitan area to Amityville; it became a mecca for an ethnically and racially diverse population drawn by desirable employment, good schools and recreation provided by the Great South Bay.

For those of us fortunate enough to have lived in Amityville in the mid-20th century, it was a great time and place to grow up. This has become more and more apparent as we grow older and pause to reflect on those wonderful years of our youth. A few years ago I learned of, and joined, a private site on Facebook dedicated to helping Amityvilleans reminisce about growing up there. No politics, no advertising, no profanity; just a place to reconnect and share stories about the good old days, the brainchild of Tommy Maher.

In 2015 I self-published a memoir about my early days in Amityville and it occurred to me that there must be a great number of wonderful, untold stories from the 2000+ members of the private Amityville website. The idea of this book, a collection of first-person stories about growing up in Amityville, was well-received by the Facebook group. Putting pen to paper was not as easy as many thought it would be, but the result is well worth the effort. Thirty individuals have contributed forty-four stories, told in their distinctive and natural voices.

This collaboration, *Growing Up in Amityville: In Their Own Words*, is available through lulu.com and other major booksellers. All proceeds from book sales go to the Amityville Historical Society.

Doug Robinson, editor
July 2021

**Many thanks to these individuals who grew up
in Amityville and contributed stories for this book.**

Debbie Becak Palmosina was born and raised in Amityville, moving on after high school. She is a grandmother now, living in Colorado, but still in close touch with many of her Amityville friends.

Steven Bogan was born and raised in Amityville, growing up on Richmond Avenue in the house where his parents still live. He attended elementary school at St. Martin of Tours and graduated from Amityville Memorial High School in 1985.

Steve Brice grew up and lived in five different houses on Ocean Avenue. After college he owned and operated Yacht Service, Inc., the last commercial entity on Ocean Avenue. He sold the business to his son who carries on the tradition.

Bruce Chattman moved to Amityville with his parents and older sister when he was three years old. He grew up in the Bailey Homes neighborhood and attended the Amityville Schools from kindergarten through graduation from high school. After graduation from college, he moved to Vermont where he still resides.

Jose (Joe) Creamer was born in Brunswick Hospital in 1950. His family moved to Connecticut in 1960. He attended Fordham University and Fordham Law School. He retired after 36 years with UPS and now lives in Milton, Georgia.

Ted Crocker grew up in Amityville, graduating from AMHS in 1973. He misses that simpler time. He currently lives in Florida and makes electric guitars for the stars, including Keith Urban and Gary Clark Jr. One of his instruments was heavily featured in the Danny Glover movie *Honeydripper*.

Lynn Darling Hendershot is the fourth generation of the Darling family to grow up in Amityville. Her great-grandfather, Oscar Darling, helped populate Amityville (and Huntington) with his 29 children.

Stephanie Deckert-Racanelli was born and raised in Amityville. Like most residents she was born in Brunswick Hospital and remained in town for close to three decades. The memories of friendships, family ties, school days and bounding fun—on and around the bay—forever remain in her heart.

Howard DeNardo lived in the Town of Oyster Bay portion of the Amityville School District and graduated from Amityville Memorial High School in 1972. He still returns to visit, especially for the football games.

Bruce Edwards moved to Amityville when he was eight months old. He attended Amityville public schools and graduated from Amityville Memorial High School in 1964. After college, he married his high school sweetheart (Susan Martin, AMHS class of 1963). They reside in Jensen Beach, Florida, and maintain a summer home in Manchester, New Hampshire.

Susan Falkenbach Welch was born in Brunswick Hospital in April, 1944 and graduated from AMHS in 1961. In 1965, her new husband taught in Amityville and she taught in West Babylon, until they moved upstate the next year. They now live on St. Augustine Beach, Florida, and in Rangeley, Maine, but have returned to her beloved Amityville to visit family and friends and attend reunions.

Maryann Ford was born in Brooklyn and moved to Amityville with her family when she was four years old. She started school at Northwest Elementary and switched to Our Lady of Lourdes through eighth grade and finished out at AMHS, graduating in 1972. She moved to New Mexico when she was 25 but has so many good memories of growing up on Long Island.

Dorothy Garvin moved with her family to Amityville, from Brooklyn, NY, in 1956. She graduated from Amityville Memorial High School in 1959, attended Molloy College, and returned to Amityville as a Social Studies teacher for 36 years. She is happily retired now, living in the home her parents purchased in 1956.

Kim Ireland grew up in Amityville in the 1940s and '50s and remembers connecting with nature on the Great South Bay and an active sports life in high school.

Katie Lynch Probst moved to Amityville with her family when she was three years old. The family moved away to upstate New York when she was in ninth grade. A retired nurse, social worker and grandmother, she still considers Amityville her home town.

Jimmy McNabb moved to Amityville when he was 15, graduating from Amityville Memorial High School in 1964. He studied Art at the University of Buffalo, the University of Sienna (Italy), and did his graduate studies at University College, London. For the last 37 years he has managed McNabb Roick Ltd., a leader in Event Design, Production and Management.

Terry Mulligan Gross moved to Amityville in 1956 when her parents bought their first home on Camp Road (which eventually became East Massapequa). A graduate of Amityville Memorial High School, class of 1971, in May, 1979, she married Donald Gross (Farmingdale) at St. Martin's Church, went on to have two sons and moved to Orange County, New York. Since retirement in 2017 Terry and Don relocated to another Bay Village, this time located on the eastern shore of Virginia, a town very similar to Amityville!

Carla Miller-Camacho was born in next-door Copiague, NY. As a late bloomer she has her B.S., MBA and MaFM and lives in Las Vegas near her family. She has written seven books including *This is Amityville Through the Music*. She is currently involved in a non-profit to assist young people seeking careers in show business.

Steve Naimoli grew up on the Amityville River with his family. He spent twenty-five years in Ft. Lauderdale as a yacht captain doing deliveries and yacht charters and recently returned to Geneva, New York, on Seneca Lake.

Carol Nehring grew up in Amityville, attending the Park Avenue schools and graduating from Amityville Memorial High School in 1964. She received a Bachelor of Fine Arts from Beaver College and worked as a book design/art director for Chanticleer Press and Reader's Digest General Books. She lives in New York City and maintains friendships with a number of Amityville friends.

Kurt Nezbeda grew up on the Great South Bay. Married to an AMHS classmate, they occasionally return to Amityville to visit family and friends.

Lou Paris moved to North Amityville in 1958 with his immediate family. After graduating from AMHS in 1963 he spent a year at Pennsylvania Military College, then left for a 35-year career in the Air Force and Air National Guard. In civilian life Lou worked as a TV news reporter and as an aircraft dispatcher at a regional airline. Currently he is an aviation safety inspector with the Federal Aviation Administration.

Betty Robinson Zion was born during a nasty Nor'easter and kept from her Ocean Avenue home by the flood tide and no electricity. Thus was her introduction to Amityville and the Great South Bay. Her family moved from Amityville in her twelfth year. She remembers those years well.

Doug Robinson spent his formative years living on Ocean Avenue in Amityville and sailing the Great South Bay. He has written three books about the town: *My Amityville, Memories of a Golden Time*, a childhood memoir; *The Golden Avenue, the History and People of Ocean Avenue, Amityville, N.Y.*; and *The Last Bayman*, a novel.

Peter Sittler was born in Amityville in 1942 and grew up there with his parents, brother, Rudy and sister, Sandy. Retired now and after three marriages, two children and three adopted children, he lives in Mississippi and stays busy with the three adopted children, rental houses and sailing.

Rudy Sittler, Jr. moved to Amityville with his family when he was three, spending his adolescence and most of his adult years there. He was closely aligned with the Narrasketuck Class of sailboats. He likes to say that his father was a true bayman but he was just a sailor.

Judy Renz Smutny grew up in Amityville and graduated high school in 1963. She attended Oneonta State and Queens Colleges receiving a masters in secondary education. She taught high school at Half Hollow Hills before moving to Miami, Florida, where she has lived for the past 42 years. She maintains several longtime friendships that were made in grade school, and will cherish them forever.

Donna Synan Tewksbury was born in Brunswick Hospital and spent her youth in Amityville. She attended St. Martin of Tours through junior high school then AMHS and the BOCES co-op program in Nursing. She pursued a career in nursing attaining the degree of Bachelor of Science in Nursing (BSN). She lives in Florida with her husband.

Virginia Synan Swartz escaped to Amityville with her family in 1951. She is married and gone from Amityville now but writing a series of amateur sleuth mysteries set in Amityville and environs, fueled by her memories of growing up there.

Brud Yates remembers the Great South Bay, sailing, digging oysters and clams with his mother, fishing with his grandfather, surfing at Gilgo Beach, and playing hockey on the canal. He graduated from AMHS in 1959, played football for Georgia Tech, coached at the Punahou School in Honolulu, and continues as a HiLevel performance coach in Hawaii.

Contents

The Influence of the Great South Bay

School Days

Sports in Amityville

Remembering Lou Howard — 183

NEIGHBORS, NEIGHBORHOODS AND FRIENDS

NEIGHBORS, NEIGHBORHOODS AND FRIENDS

THE BAILEY HOMES

by Bruce Chattman !!!

For many of us, growing up in Amityville coincided with the excitement and energy of the post-WWII era and the expansion of the American Dream made possible by the corresponding economic boom. We were born into a community that thrived for generations on self-sufficiency related to fertile lands, with a bay created by several off-shore barrier islands full of clams, crabs, fluke, perch, flounder and blue fish (remember the rush of catching snappers?). A little further out through the island inlets was the Atlantic Ocean with larger versions of the bay fish, striped and sea bass, porgies, dolphin and for the adventuresome—tuna and shark. Proximity to beautiful bay and ocean beaches and easy access from Amityville via the southern LIRR train "route of the dashing commuter" to Brooklyn and New York City resulted in Amityville also becoming home for many business professionals, entrepreneurs and business owners. Canals were built to accommodate beautiful homes with easy water access and Amityville also had an active summer population from the city regions.

The robust economy of the post WWII generation spurred by the GI Bill with subsidies for mortgages, the baby boom with expanding families, the development of interstate highways and the growth of the middle class resulted in the establishment of new suburbs in eastern Nassau and Suffolk Counties. Because of the Long Island Rail Road and its close connection to natural resources, Amityville expanded from the south shore core of original homes and businesses to the north side of the Village. This expansion replaced the farms, fields and woods located north of the established village with new single-family constructed homes quickly built with the new technology of mass production and efficient designs, mostly ranch, cape and split levels. During the early years of expansion, there was no mass transit to connect people from these new neighborhoods with the Village. There were also no neighborhood schools and the Village of Amityville was a 5+ mile walk or bike ride down County Line Road or one of the other two-lane country roads, lined by trees and forests. All routes to town included the challenge of crossing Sunrise Highway (Route 27), a fast and congested road with no traffic lights or crossing lines.

As Amityville expanded and evolved, it retained its rich cultural history and melded into its new identity smoothly, largely because of the important role of the Amityville School System as a common thread for assimilation and amalgamation of new residents, especially for the children and youth, who settled in the new "suburbs" of Amityville in the '40s, '50s and early '60s. The only public schools for Amityville prior to 1953 were on Park Avenue, including the junior high school and high school. In 1953 a new high school was opened on Merrick Road and the Park Avenue schools were realigned to accommodate the increasing K–8 student population.

Because all the children of Amityville, including those in the new neighborhoods, attended the schools on Park Avenue, people of different cultures, religions, races, and ethnicity were in the same schools and classes. The only exception was those families who chose to send their children to Saint Martin of Tours School, an elementary Catholic school on Union Avenue.

I grew up in one of these new neighborhoods—The Bailey Homes, named for the developer. It consisted of three short streets: Plymouth Drive, Bailey Drive and Francine Avenue. Francine Avenue split and had both a north and south loop called S. Francine Drive and N. Francine Drive. Robert Avenue dissected these streets, essentially making them only two blocks long. The neighborhood, upon completion, had about 130 homes on small lots of a quarter acre or less. During the following decades, the Amityville schools received and educated hundreds of students from this neighborhood. Bailey Homes was an isolated neighborhood defined by two north-south roads (Carmen Road and County Line Road) that provided the west and east borders. These two roads, heavily wooded between Southern State Parkway on the north and Sunrise Highway on the south, were built creating a wonderful opportunity for youthful adventures of exploration, fantasy and fun.

My parents bought their newly constructed cape-style home on Robert Avenue in 1948, when I was three years old and until about the time I was 10, we remained an isolated neighborhood until the forests north and south of us became additional neighborhoods due to the continued development of the region. During these early formative years, my peer group consisted of the kids around my age who lived in the Bailey Homes. My core group consisted of Norman Sonne, Phil Kellogg, Bob and Diane Dau, Jane Schlichtemeier, Rich Staab, Charlie Makula and, for a few years until he moved, Jimmy Decker. These friends also had older and younger siblings who would occasionally join with us for events such as block parties or group games such as Red Rover, Hide and Seek, and Tag. Because there were no local neighborhood schools at that time, our activities were neighborhood based and this is where we developed close bonds that have lasted until today.

Like with all close friends, we had a lot of fun with the occasional "I'll never talk to you again" moments that might last as long as two or three hours, maybe overnight if it happened late in the day. Fun was playing baseball in the streets with the four corners at the intersection of Robert Avenue and Bailey Drive as our infield. My Dad, who coached Little League, suggested that home plate be at the corner in front of our home as he didn't want to be the recipient of the occasional broken window. Obviously, playing on pavement had its advantages and disadvantages with the major advantage being the predictable bounce and speed of the grounders on pavement. The biggest disadvantage—sliding into home plate, but that did not deter us at all. Our moms had lots of iodine and bandages. The pitcher was always Norman Sonne. Norm had the best arm in the neighborhood and deadly aim. (I often think that baseball was just Norm's way of staying in shape for the winter snowball fights when the intended target would be anyone within throwing range.)

As we got older, the occasional "won't talk to you again" moments became physical with pushing, shoving, wrestling and an occasional fist fight until one of us said "give." We didn't usually want to seriously hurt each other. However, I recall one such fight on a Saturday morning when I was about 9 and adult intervention was needed. We often gathered in a small group to watch cowboy TV shows and movies before our Saturday afternoon baseball game. This fascination with the old west resulted in our sometimes playing "Cowboys and Indians" where we dressed the part with cowboy shirts and hats, toy guns, Indian headdresses with feathers and actual bows and arrows purchased at a 5&10 store. (We even drank water from the hose and rode in the back of trucks.)

On one particular Saturday, we were encouraged to go outside and play, probably because it was a nice day and the host parent decided we needed fresh air. After dressing for our parts, we reconvened and found our allotted hiding places throughout the neighborhood for the "stalking of the enemy" phase of the game. Because Norm was one of the "Indians," I chose to hide in the bushes behind his house thinking I would surprise him as he came out. However, as I hid and waited he left his house by the front door sneaking through the front yard bushes of his next-door neighbor's house that separated his house from mine. Upon determining that I was not hiding around my house, he quietly circled around behind me.

Upon seeing me, he let out a war hoop and shot his arrow from about 25 feet away, hitting me in my arm. We were used to being hit by the arrows but they had dull tin tips and seldom penetrated our clothing, but I was wearing a short-sleeved shirt and blood flowed down my arm adding a sense of reality to our game.

I wasn't hurt but became angry, more so for being found by him than by his aim, and I charged with my weapon to engage him in Indian and Cowboy man-to-man mock combat. As I got closer to him, Norm saw the blood on my arm and thought it great fun to mock and taunt me, only fueling my anger, resulting in a chase around the neighborhood. He was faster than I was but tired of running after a while and I finally caught up to him about six houses down the street and we began to fight. When Norm said "give," it only escalated my anger and my toy cowboy pistol became a weapon; I was no longer "playing." As I raised my pistol to club him on the head, I felt my arm grabbed and a loud voice said "STOP! Stop it right now!" None other than my second mother, Evelyn Sonne, Norm's mother, pulled me off of Norm. Evidently one of the other Cowboys or Indians alerted her to the fight. Both of us were escorted back to my house where I was turned over to my mom while Norm was dragged home by his. Norm's last parting words were "I'll never play with you again." Late that afternoon, after intervention by our mothers, I called Norm and apologized and we ended the day with a sleep over. "Never" is a word that didn't last long among good friends.

As we reached the size when we were big enough that home runs became frequent, we were also old enough to join Little League. Little League became the main way in which we occupied ourselves during the summer afternoon and evenings. Little League, in addition to Amityville Elementary School, was one of the few ways that we were able to expand our network of friends beyond the neighborhood. Interestingly, the names of the teams had the names from the Iroquois Nation - Cayugas, Oneidas, Mohawks, and Senecas. In retrospect, I wonder if this was not intentional to connect the little league with the AMHS Warrior logo.

Little League and school became very significant mirrors of the world because they were major places where we interacted with folks outside of the Bailey Homes. Little Leaguers came from homes throughout town, from those south of the LIRR and located along the canals off the bay or in close proximity thereof. Others came from the well-established beautiful homes on Bayview Avenue, Avon Place and the close environs of Amityville Village while we came from north of Sunrise Highway.

Because there were no "neighborhood schools" in the '40s and '50s, our schools were integrated and one of my favorite teachers in elementary school was Miss Hunter, an African American. In Little League, as in the schools, there were people of color and different ethnicities, not found in the Bailey Homes. We grew up thinking that "normal" was what we saw and experienced every day. Even the (non-school associated) AMHS high school fraternity (AOT) was comprised of people of different races and ethnicity. But we didn't think in these terms then, these were just our schoolmates and friends. My ignorance that there were racial issues within Amityville hit me hard while away for my freshman year in college as I read of the lawsuits for de-facto segregation in Amityville. It was then that I learned that the NE Elementary and NW Elementary Schools in Amityville, that opened in 1959, resulted in segregating the people who lived in these neighbor-hoods—neighborhoods developed systemically by race throughout Long Island, including Amityville.

As we got older and the testosterone began to kick in, sports became our primary focus in the Bailey Homes. The males within the core group of my friends found many ways to let off steam. During our pre- and early-teens, we decided that boxing would be fun. Bob Dau's dad put up both a punching bag and a speed bag in his garage and also had some free weights available. We would "train" there and put on the gloves in the basement of Rich's house, which served as our boxing "ring." There, we would take turns seeing who could take the most punches because defense was not a skill that came naturally. While there was no "Champion" ever determined, we all felt like winners because we all were able to both take and deliver a good shot. As we moved into grades seven and eight, we began to play football. There were no Pop Warner Leagues but we played a modified game in middle school and played contact football among ourselves on the new athletic field at the recently built NW Elementary School field during summers. It was there that we met Roland "Skip" Hepburn, who had moved into the newer homes built south of the Bailey Homes. Skip was later to become a quarterback for the varsity team. The rest of us went on to become starters on the high school football team for classes of 1960–1963. While we all had football in common, we were diverse in our winter and spring sport of choice. Norm and Skip played basketball. Bob, Rich, Charlie and I were on the wrestling team. In the spring, Bob, Norm, Rich and I were on the track team, with me taking a hiatus my junior year. During this hiatus, I joined the tennis team where I played first doubles with Doug Robinson, our best player. Needless to say, he carried me.

Neighbors, Neighborhoods and Friends

THE SUMP

by Howard DeNardo

Growing up in Amityville was an amazing part of my life. Being a baby boomer, the whole neighborhood was the same age group and that was just unbelievable. We played together as a block and you knew everyone on your block. You also knew all the neighboring blocks. We had Ford Drive South, Camp Road, Soloff Road, Joyce Ave., and Ford Drive West just to name a few. To this day I can still tell you all the family names of everyone who lived on my street. Over a couple of beers in a local pub at my new home in Florida, I told my Buddies this. They took me up on it and off I went naming them all. They were truly amazed. This was followed by hours of reminiscing about life in the Bay Village.

Not only did you know all the kids within a mile radius, but you knew their parents too. What was even better was the fact that they knew you. You constantly were under the neighborhood watch. If you were out of line, they were quick to give you a smack on the butt without fear of reprisal from your parents. This went a long way to keep us in line. Well, almost.

The blocks were like tribes. They had chiefs, beautiful squaws, and warriors. You all knew who you were if you lived here. As we got older, it got to be competitive. We played baseball, hockey, football, and stickball against each other. Northwest School yard was the place to be growing up. It was our arena. We all congregated there to enjoy the day and by day this usually meant from the crack of dawn to when the street lights came on. We had the handball courts, baseball fields,

The Sump today, courtesy of Google Maps.

basketball courts, and huge open fields where any sport could be played.

We would play baseball on a makeshift field utilizing the school yard fence behind Camp Road as the outfield wall. Select players going hand over hand on a baseball bat to pick teams. Do you remember that? My weapon of mass destruction was a Ross Moschitto Louisville Slugger I got at bat day at Yankee Stadium. This was our Yankee Stadium. We would dream of hitting it over the fence for a homer. Unfortunately, not all the home owners who lived there enjoyed our play. We had to have skilled fence climbers who would retrieve those monster home runs with lightning speed before they were spotted by the residents. Otherwise the ball would be lost forever... And for the Mickey Mantles of the neighborhood, which there were many, if you the hit a house, it was game over.

Living on Ford Drive South had another advantage. It was called "The Sump." They were built for drainage control of water run-off from our streets. They were sanctuaries protected by barbed wire fences and "No Trespassing" signs governed by the Town of Oyster Bay. It was surrounded by shrubbery to make it more aesthetic for the community. For us, it was a wonderland. It was a sand pit surrounded by sand walls with a grass perimeter on top. It was perfect. The shrubbery provided cover for us to cut the fence so we could slither in and explore this new sport venue. It was home to the best games of tag, army, hide and seek, and red rover you could ever imagine. The manhole and drainage pipes provided us with a vast underground labyrinth to explore if you dared. To this day, I can't believe we roamed through those small drainage pipes. We used to use manhole covers on storm drains on our street for bases during Ringolevio. I still remember hands coming out the front of the storm drain touching the base and yelling "free all" from the drain explorers of which I was one.

The winter brought a whole different persona to The Sump. It became home to the Winter Olympics! Snowball fights and snow forts. Sleigh riding was king on the hills of The Sump. Snurfing (snow surfing) championships were held on the hills as well. Unbelievable times and memories where made on those hills. The floor of The Sump when filled with water would freeze. Then the skating events were held there. Girls figure skating would be going on at one end. The block ice hockey championships were held at the other. Many of us learned to skate in the arena called The Sump.

With the coming of spring, tadpoles would become toads and The Sump would be filled with these amazing creatures. The toad hunters of the block would come in droves to catch them and bring them home as pets. Box turtles that are very rarely seen today would also be trophy catches.

As years went on and sewers were put in, The Sump became dry. The boys of the block decided that The Sump would be the future home of our softball games. We all worked hard for two weeks to transfer the floor of The Sump to a baseball diamond. We cut out the infield and even put clay down. We built a mound complete with a pitching rubber. We all used the family mowers to cut the outfield grass. Just like in the movie "if you build it they will come," came true. Block teams would play each other for the crown for about a month. One day for some reason the Town of Oyster Bay Public Works showed up and closed down our stadium. No more games were ever played but the memories will last forever.

During my high school years it became a den of inequity. Our initiation to beer began here. We would sneak our parents' beverage of choice under the cover of darkness into the depths of The Sump to consume. It didn't take long before our parents caught on and even the local police began to patrol The Sump. So many people were sworn to secrecy during these times at The Sump bar and grill.

In Amityville, the football teams were legendary. Every young man wanted to be a member of The Tide. No weight rooms back then. I remember pushing my Dad's station wagon with my brother steering, out the driveway and the back, to build my strength. My leg work was accomplished by running the hills in The Sump with a 50-pound weight vest to get ready for the big boys at practice. As a 5'7", 155-lb. lineman everybody else was a big boy! I owe some of the best times of my life playing with some of the best athletes I ever saw to those Sump hills and I'm forever grateful!

Last year I returned to the scene of the crime. Our glorious Sump is nothing more than an overgrown sand pit. Trees now grow out of the hills that were the scene of some of the best sleigh rides of my life. Snurfers would no longer navigate the hills here. The floor of The Sump is indistinguishable. Some of the best hockey and ball games ever played as a boy are hard to comprehend; of ever being able to

That's me on the left with Paul Reagan in 1977. The Sump is over Paul's left shoulder.

be played here.

The memories are all that remain of an era when kids could be kids. Never was an adult coach present. There weren't any participation trophies either. It was just a bunch of neighborhood kids forming teams or choosing sides and doing what kids do. Forming bonds that last a lifetime, making memories, and having just plain fun!

I didn't mention names in this little blurb but you all know who you are. Thanks for making memories.

NEIGHBORS, NEIGHBORHOODS AND FRIENDS

LOST INNOCENCE

by Terry Mulligan Gross

The homes along Camp Road were constructed in one of the many new neighborhoods built on Long Island in the mid-1950s to accommodate the population shift from the boroughs of New York City to the suburbs. The development consisted of a number of streets intertwined with houses built on lots the size of small squares. Number 11 Camp Road was home for my family! Deceptively larger than the house appeared from the outside, it masked a four-level floor plan that consisted of four bedrooms, one and a half baths, a family room (we called it the playroom), the living room, dining room, and kitchen. For a young couple with four small children, this house seemed perfect. But in time four more children would come along, causing it almost to burst!

Our neighborhood quickly filled with other families. It wasn't long before everyone knew each other. Roads were paved, cement sidewalks were poured, and an elementary school built. This wasn't unique; it was happening all over Long Island. Neighborhoods, school districts, shopping centers, and houses of worship were springing up on fields that once grew potatoes. Life couldn't be better!

Those were the days of the milk man, the bread man, the ice cream man, and even a guy who had a huge grinder on the back of his truck that he used to sharpen knives and scissors. Most families had only one car, so these services were brought in. Very few mothers worked outside the home; very few fathers did not. We kids were always playing outdoors. Friendships grew as fast as the lawns and flowers that were planted. On summer evenings, after the street lights came on, kids would return to their homes but continued to play in their front yards until it got good and dark. Catching fireflies, playing flashlight tag and statue on the lawn were common sights, while the adults sat chatting on folding chairs in nearby driveways.

Kids were everywhere! Baseball was played in the street with shouts of "Car!" yelled as warning when an automobile approached. Bicycles were the mode of transportation and the distinctive click-click sound of a baseball card fastened to the tire spoke using a clothes pin was the rage. Games like potsy, jump rope, and flipping baseball cards were just some of the fun ways we would pass the time. The grounds that surrounded Northwest Elementary School provided a playground, baseball fields, a handball court, and lots of open space to explore. But what attracted us most, though, was the area beyond the school yard.

This attraction consisted of a huge grassy field lined by woods with a small, shallow creek that rambled along its edge. While most neighborhood mothers deemed it taboo to play there, the lure of woods and water pulled us in. It wasn't just building forts, dams and bridges in the creek, or the freedom to explore that intrigued us, there was a mystery and legend that made it feel daring and dangerous. Further back behind the woods stood the grounds to South Oaks Hospital, a large psychiatric facility. If the fact that the woods bordered a mental hospital wasn't enough to scare us, the legend of the Watch Guard added a whole other layer to our fears. The truth is that the Watch Guard we feared was nothing more than the grounds maintenance man who worked at the hospital!

South Oaks was a large facility with a number of buildings spread out over acres of land that extended on both sides of Sunrise Highway. A truck was provided for the maintenance employee to use in order to get around, but to us he was there to patrol the property and capture children he caught playing in the woods. Stories were told of kids who supposedly got caught and those who never returned,

11 Camp Road on Christmas Day, riding our new bikes.

lending an air of daring adventure to our play.

All of us kids looked out for each other and it wasn't uncommon to hear shouts of "Watch Guard" as warning whenever he was spied getting into his truck. Those within earshot could be seen scurrying to take cover and hide. Crouched down in bushes and hearing the truck getting closer and closer, we were convinced that he saw us and we were doomed! But he never stopped, he barely seemed to notice us as he drove by. This man had a job to do and probably cared less about us, that is until one particular day.

It was summer and kids were playing in the field while others were floating sticks in the creek. Some were riding their bikes, while another group was having a picnic. We must have been too distracted that day to notice that the Watch Guard had started his truck, steering off the path and was headed our way. Shouts of warning echoed through the air as kids began to scatter. Suddenly, the truck abruptly came to a halt and the Watch Guard jumped out and started chasing us on foot! My heart pounded through my chest as I ran as fast as I could towards the opening in the fence that ensured safety, not daring to look back. Kids pushed and shoved to make it through to the "safe" side. Once safe, we gathered on the sidewalk trying to recover from the ordeal. Versions of the story were told many times in the months to come, the details more exaggerated with each telling. In one scenario a boy claimed the Watch Guard caught hold of his shirt and it ripped when he pulled away. Others claimed he growled like a bear as he removed his belt and started swinging it like a whip! Each tale further escalated the element of danger to our lives!

Unfortunately, danger did exist in those woods, and it surfaced some 20 years later. The peril wasn't from a Watch Guard, or a patient at South Oaks, or a stranger lurking nearby; it came in the form of a friend, someone the victim trusted. The murder of 11-year-old Angela Wong shocked everyone. An adorable, popular young girl, Angela was the daughter of long-time Amityville residents and the granddaughter of one of the original families to live on Camp Road. Angela's mother and uncles played in those woods as kids, never imagining the horror that would someday touch their lives.

In the summer of 1984 the woods became a popular shortcut to the nearby Sunrise Mall that had opened a few years prior. Angela had spent the day in the family garage with her brother and his pals who were preparing for a break dance competition. By late afternoon, she was seen walking with her brother until they parted ways. He went in one direction, she in the opposite. By the following day, her body was found deep in the woods on the banks of the creek— her clothing in disarray, her face bruised, and her head underwater, weighed down by a heavy log. The neighborhood was stunned that this could happen in broad daylight, virtually in their backyards. Even more shocking was the fact that it was a family friend, someone who Angela knew and trusted. It took police 18 years to secure enough evidence, and it was their diligence that led to the arrest of a friend of Angela's brother, one of the young boys in the garage on that fateful day. In 2004, he was convicted and is currently serving time for murder and sexual assault.

Like much of Long Island, the area has changed. South Oaks sold that piece of property and condos have been built. The woods have been thinned out and while the field is still there, it's not the neighborhood amusement hub it once was. Ironically, the thought that has often entered my mind since that summer day in 1984 is this: the realization that had the Watch Guard still been making rounds he might have been the one to save Angela.

The imaginary fears we faced while playing in those woods all those years ago have since become heightened and real. The shortcut is no longer used. Kids don't play outdoors with the freedom they once did. Much like the bread man, the milk man and the guy sharpening knives, the innocence of that time and place is now a thing of the past.

IT ONLY COST TEN CENTS

by Lou Paris

In the early 1960s in Amityville we were too young to drive so we walked or rode our bikes everywhere. My "crew" consisted of Bernard Myers, Bob Hunt, Mike Fields, George Johnson, me, and sometimes Lou Mosley. We spent many Saturday nights walking to various places around North Amityville, usually to house parties.

Then, as now, teenagers are full of mischief. One of our favorite tricks was to pick a random number from the telephone book (remember them?). We'd write the number down, go to the nearest pay phone, insert a dime (or short-circuit the receiver), and call the number…usually beginning about 9 p.m. Remember…there were no answering machines back then. People actually answered their phones. When the disembodied voice answered one of us would say something like, "Is Lou Paris there?" Of course, the person, not knowing who Lou Paris was, would answer, "There's no one here by that name." We'd then say, "Well, if he calls tell him Bernard called." We'd repeat this scenario about once an hour, always asking for Lou Paris (or whoever's name we chose that night) and leaving a message with another name.

When we were ready to go home for the night one of us would call the number (by this time it was usually about 1 a.m.), and say something like, "This is Lou Paris. Are there any messages for me?"

You can imagine the responses…some of them not so pleasant.

NEIGHBORS, NEIGHBORHOODS AND FRIENDS

THREE MEMORIES

by Bruce Edwards

One of my fondest memories of Amityville took place when John "Butch" Bousquet and I borrowed Seaford Skiff #2 from its owner, Kurt Nezbeda, and decided we would race in the regular Sunday afternoon sailboat races. The further out we sailed, the worse the sky was becoming. By the time we reached the staging area, there was a dead calm which turned out to be the true "calm before the storm." Soon rain came down as fast and as furious as I had ever witnessed. The wind came next in strong gusts, and we were not only soaked and miserable, but were now freezing from the wind which had us chilled to the bone. We decided to abort before the race began and headed back to Kurt's dock. Since Butch was the skipper, I decided I had had enough and managed to get myself under the deck of the Seaford Skiff to ride out the storm. He did everything he could to get me to change places with him but I wasn't moving. I will never forget the look on his face as he made his plea! I don't believe either one of us ever raced again.

. . . .

The sandlot next door to the Robinsons' Ocean Avenue home was a truly great place to play until Mr. Bernagozi (a local home builder) decided to build several homes in our play area. I remember climbing around on one of the newly framed homes when my friend, Doug Robinson, cracked one of the ceiling joists on which he was climbing.

The Robert Wheeler family lived in that home for many years after until my in-laws (Eleanor and Humbert Martin Jr.) purchased that very same house. Every time I would sit in the dining room, which was the location of the cracked joist, I would wonder if that cracked joist had ever been replaced!

One summer in our early teen years (too young to get a work permit), Courtley Lottman and I decided we would dig clams for extra money. We headed out to Sand Island one morning and proceeded to fill the rear portion of my dad's 15-foot Lyman outboard runabout. All of our clams were taken "by foot" and without the benefit of rakes. After a good sized clam lunch, we headed back to the mainland on what should have been a 15 minute trip. It turned out that the trip took 40 minutes because the poorly distributed weight of the clams wouldn't allow the boat to plane and we were too stubborn to take the time to redistribute the weight. We sold our clams for 30 cents per dozen while cherrystones went for 40 cents. We did pretty well that day.

DEWEY

by Terry Mulligan Gross

Ask any "Baby Boomer" what the sound of ringing bells on a hot summer day calls to mind and I think they would agree: The ice cream man is coming! Ask that same question to any adult over age 50 who grew up in Amityville, particularly in the Northwest section of town, and the answer is sure to be the ice cream man everyone called Dewey! Guaranteed!

During the late 1950s, '60s and '70s there were a couple of ice cream vendors competing for our nickels and dimes. None, however, left a lifelong impression as strong as Dewey's. There was Bungalow Bar: You would hear the kids chant, "Bungalow Bar tastes like tar…" as his truck drove by. We also had Mister Softee, but his truck always came later at night and his special soft-serve custard seemed to appeal more to adults. But it was Good Humor that all the neighborhood kids wanted and it wasn't our loyalty to their brand that sold us, it was the driver, Dewey we loved.

I cannot remember a summer that Dewey didn't make the rounds. At first, it was his little white truck with its open cab and an insulated boxed back portion that had compartments on all three sides. Each side had a heavy latched door that, when opened, exposed huge chunks of dry ice along with an assortment of ice cream novelties. Bells were strung above the windshield with a cord that extended long enough to pull with one hand while the other grasped the steering wheel. Eventually Dewey drove a bigger box truck with a large open window on the side that enabled him to move from the driver's seat to the serving counter without having to step outside. Dewey was a smaller framed man but larger than life as he stood high above us from his perch. His distinctive southern twang almost made him sound as if he was singing when he talked. He wore the requisite white shirt, creased pants, hat, and the trademark silver coin holder around his waist. He seemed ageless, an adult but almost a contemporary, one of us! We had no idea where he lived or what he did in the winter months but I remember someone once telling us that he was married with children of his own and I covered my ears because I didn't want to hear it! We were his children and Dewey was ours and ours alone!

His truck seemed to be everywhere, as if it were magical. Ride your bike down to the Little League field and there would be Dewey pulled over in the parking lot, selling ice cream and peeking to watch part of the game. Walk with your friends to choir practice, blocks from home and there you would see his truck making the rounds through that neighborhood. I can remember watching as the back of his truck drove down Smith Street, on the opposite side of Route 110 in the direction of North Amityville where the black people lived and realizing that no place was off limits to Dewey.

Like Santa Claus, he seemed to know just where to go at just the right time. When the bells of his truck were heard in the distance kids would scurry to their homes pleading, "Mom, can we get Dewey???" No one called it ice cream, it was Dewey! A dreaded response was to hear, "No, we have ice cream in the freezer!" What most moms didn't understand was that it wasn't just the ice cream, it was the whole experience. The thrill of being the one to yell, "STOP", reading the picture menu on display showing all the Good Humor treats… The Chocolate Bar with either vanilla or chocolate ice cream and the chocolate shell covering, the Chocolate Éclair, the Toasted Almond, the Strawberry Shortcake on a stick…it was a tough choice! Even kids who weren't buying would gather around and Dewey would joke with us all. Some names he remembered but mostly he called us by little nicknames and I realize now that he probably used those same nicknames over and over in every neighborhood but it always made me feel special when he called me "freckles." There were special occasions to be celebrated and Dewey would join in. If you were one of the lucky ones to have a summer birthday you got a free ice cream! If you got your tonsils out during the summer Dewey would park his truck and bring ice cream to you. Sometimes he would even let you ring the bells or push the lever on his coin changer.

Many years have passed and I'm not sure what happened to Dewey, or when he actually stopped coming around. Recently a Facebook page was established for all those who grew up in Amityville. Many have shared memories, old photos and stories of times gone by. Favorite teachers, favorite hang-outs, famous politicians that visited our town but the memory that has sparked the most comments is the post about Dewey. Kids who grew up in those wonderful years of the '50s, '60s, and '70s have shared their stories. Three decades of kids were touched by this simple ice cream man. Someone posted that Dewey had passed away a number of years ago. I covered my ears because I didn't want to hear it! Dewey will forever be ours and ours alone!

THE FOURTH OF JULY

by Katie Lynch Probst

I remember being a little kid in Amityville, New York, in the '60s. It was like that show *The Wonder Years*. The whole town showed up for the annual 4th of July Parade. Lost in a sea of red, white, and blue, we stood on the sidewalk, waving our little American flags, feeling very patriotic.

My favorite was always the bagpipers. Dressed in their red plaid kilts, with their big furry hats, I thought they were some kind of storybook characters and I cried when they passed.

Afterward, we would go to the Amityville Beach and try and find a little plot of sand to call our own for the day. We had a thermos of lemonade and a basket packed with sandwiches, fruit, and cookies. I remember all the smells of all the different food; tuna, peanut butter, peaches, all mingled together with Coppertone, salty air, and sweat.

Since it was the town beach, we all knew each other. We saw the same faces, year after year. Mothers chatted with each other, dads drank beer and read the paper. The kids splashed in the salty, seaweed-laden bay and begged for ice cream or french fries from the concession stand.

The way home was never fun. Having to carry everything back to the car, wet bathing suit full of sand, itching sun burn, and sticky faces. We were sent to take a bath, and then a nap so we'd be awake for the fireworks. This gave the parents some time to rest and drink some adult cocktails in the afternoon.

Then in fresh clothes and armed with our sparklers, it was back to the beach to watch the fireworks. We all sat on the hoods of our cars, necks craned, "oohing and ahhhing" for the next hour as beautiful explosive lights rained colors down upon us. Magical!!! That was 4th of July in Amityville, when I was growing up.

PEGGY 'N' ME

by Debbie Becak Palmosina

I first met Peggy McConlogue on the bus for our first day of kindergarten in 1955. Her family lived on Breezy Point, just a short walk from our house on Carmen Boulevard. That was in the western part of Amityville, actually in Nassau County. It is East Massapequa now.

We became fast friends and through our friendship our parents became friends as well.

Peggy lived on the water; the McConlogue house backed up to the canal that made Breezy Point an island. We both loved being around and on the water. So much so that, at age eleven, we decided we wanted to have our own boat. Peggy pressed her mom and dad about it and they agreed, under two conditions. First we had to earn half the cost of the boat and second, we had to take a course in boating safety.

We both worked hard to get the money we needed—mostly doing yard work for our families and neighbors. We ended up buying an eight-foot dinghy with a 3 1/2 horse outboard and kept it at Peggy's house. We both took the U.S. Coast Guard course in small boat safety.

Boy did we think we were Hot Stuff. During the summers, after swimming lessons at the Amityville Beach, we spent every afternoon out in that boat. The canal took us out to the Great South Bay and we would putter around, exploring the waterfront, just singing away. Peggy's mom said she was not worried because she always knew where we were; we were so loud she could hear us out on the water, invariably singing our favorite song by the Angels—"My boyfriend's back and you're gonna be in trouble/ hey-na-na-na, my boyfriend's back."

Peggy's family moved to Bayport, out on Long Island, after junior high and I ended up in Colorado after high school. We still keep in touch, buds for life. We talked the other day and laughed about our boat and our singing. She still has the certificate from the boating course, tucked away safely in her wallet. It is still valid today like our memories of growing up in Amityville.

LETTERS FROM "DA VILLE," PART I

by Lou Paris

It was June of 1960 when the "F" on my report card portended that it was going to be a long summer. At that point in my life World History was not high on my list of projected summer activities. Mom wasn't happy. My father was only concerned about the high price, 25 dollars, of the makeup summer school class.

As it turns out my friend, Gregory Acosta, also needed a summer school class. Since there were no summer courses offered at Amityville Memorial High School we both registered for the courses we needed at Massapequa Park High School. On most days my mother drove us to the Long Island Railroad Station in "the Ville" so we could take the one-stop ride to Massapequa Park.

The LIRR conductors usually waited until passengers found a seat before collecting fares from those who hadn't prepaid. Greg and I came up with a brilliant plan. We could get on the train in Amityville at the back, slowly walk toward the front, and by the time we got to the lead car the three-minute train ride to Massapequa Park would be over, and we'd save the 25-cent fare. We would do the same on the return trip. On most days it worked.

It's only recently that I shared that story with our friend, Frank Aikman. His dad was a vice president of the LIRR at the time.

LETTERS FROM "DA VILLE," PART II

by Lou Paris

Those of us who grew up in Amityville, New York, in the late '50s and early '60s often reminisce about the "good old days." However, for many of us "Amityville" was just our postal address…we really didn't live there at all. The only legal connection we had to Amityville was the school district.

While some considered the Long Island Railroad tracks the boundary, the north end of the village actually ended at Smith Street…about a mile north of the tracks. Most of the Black population lived north of Smith Street and east of Broadway. This was the other Amityville. North Amityville was not a legal entity. It was just an unincorporated area in the town of Babylon. The Amityville Village Police Department didn't patrol there. We were overseen by the Town of Babylon (later Suffolk County) police force. The Amityville Village Fire Department didn't come to our aid. We relied on the North Amityville Volunteer Fire Department.

North Amityville was its own ecosystem. That's not to say that we didn't interact with people and businesses on the south side of the Long Island Railroad tracks, but we had our own world. When we needed a tooth filled we went to Doctor Reed at the Croydon Medical Center. Same if we had appendicitis…we made an appointment with Doctor G. Harold Kopchinski (a Black man) at Croydon. Need gas? We went to the Ronek Servicenter at the corner of Albany Avenue and Great Neck Road, owned by the family of my best friend, Bernard Myers. Have the desire for a good movie? It was off to the All-Weather Drive In on Sunrise Highway. When we needed groceries, we went to Hills on Broadway or the Associated on "the corner" (that's another story).

When we wanted to party, we went to "the dugout," which was actually the home of the Black American Legion Post. It was called the dugout because it was only a basement…no upper floors had been built at that time. There was a White American Legion Post south of the tracks in "the village." At that time, I didn't really understand the dichotomy. When the grown folks wanted to party they went to Anson's.

When you needed religion you went to Hollywood Baptist, Bethel AME, or any of the myriad churches north and east of the tracks.

We went to high school in "the village." We were overjoyed in 1961 when the first ever Black teacher arrived. Marius Region taught biology and was an inspiration to many of us.

North Amityville was, indeed, a different world.

THREE AMIGAS, FRIENDS FOR LIFE

by Donna Synan Tewksbury

It was the spring of my sophomore year at Amityville Memorial High School in 1971. My father had heard that BOCES (Boards of Cooperative Educational Services), the trade school, was coming to do interviews at the high school for training for the Licensed Practical Nurse (LPN) program. His sister, my aunt Mary, was a registered nurse, trained in New York City at St. Vincent's Hospital. I was number seven of nine children in my family and my dad used to say, kiddingly, "You're the only Synan in the bunch." I think I reminded him of his sister so he chose me to be the one to be the nurse. I said OK.

I remember the interviews were held in the guidance office. I had this favorite butter-yellow sweater set. I was a skinny little thing so could wear anything. I loved that outfit; it was classic 1970s—a short-sleeve top with an embroidered flower in the center of the chest, and a miniskirt. I wore it with clunky-heeled black shoes to meet with the head of the Nursing program.

I came to the high school from St. Martin of Tours and, being Catholic School educated, found I could keep a good GPA without trying very hard. I needed an 85 average for the nursing program which was not an issue. I was accepted and that started my journey in nursing which took me to my current position of Registered Nurse, Bachelor of Science in Nursing (RN, BSN).

My story of two friendships, a special threesome, began that year.

I knew Marion Marcley since kindergarten. In fact, we are sitting next to each

At the beach in Montauk. From L to R, Kathy O'Connell Russo, Marion Marcley Johnson and Donna Synan Tewksbury—the Three Amigas.

other in the photo of Mrs. Rau's kindergarten class at Park Avenue School. So maybe it was destiny that she saw me in the hall one day in 1971 and asked, "Hey, are you going to the LPN program at BOCES?" I told her my story and that I would be interviewing. We both got in.

We wore blue pinstripe button-down dresses that came to our knees and hair tied up in a bun. They called me Olive Oil for obvious reasons. It was the beginning of a friendship that has lasted to this day. Our friend Kathy O'Connell, who we knew since ninth grade, was also going to "Tech," (also known as Lewis A. Wilson School of Practical Nursing). Kathy was our girl for learning all the things that public school unofficially taught; like smoking and drinking and other stuff. She became the third of our trio: the Three Amigas.

We would talk about boys and listen to everything from Carol King's "Tapestry," James Taylor's "Fire and Rain," Van Morrison's "St. Dominic's Preview" or Simon and Garfunkel, all the way to "Stairway to Heaven" and Don McLean's "American Pie." We were each other's confidants, gave each other advice and Marion, mostly, kept us out of trouble. I remember going to Mass together before school for Lent, then stopping in at Al's Deli for a buttered roll and an orange juice. Marion is still our voice of reason today and we love each other very much. We have been through many trials and tribulations together and, like true sisters (I have five, Marion has five) we have had our differences but, respectfully, are able to have good faith conversations.

Amityville brought us together. Marion married Jim Johnson (Johnson Butcher). Kathy is in South Carolina with her husband, Joe, and I live in Florida with my husband, Craig, but we all see each other and Zoom when we can. We get together every September and stay at The Wavecrest in Montauk. Still hanging out at the ocean, like we did summers at Gilgo, watching the waves roll in.

THE SAD TIMES

by Steve Brice with help from his sisters Phyllis, DeeDee, and Marcia

Back in the early 1960s, I was in junior high school with three older teenage sisters and one younger sister. During this time, we were deeply touched by the tragedies of others in the community.

My oldest sister, Phyllis, used to date Kevin Carty, but at this time he was dating a friend of hers. Kevin's brother had died a few years earlier as a passenger in a car headed home from college. Then Kevin's mother contracted cancer and he visited her every day…except one, which turned out to be the day she died. After dropping off my sister's friend, he lost control of his car on South Bayview and Merrick Road and died from injuries he sustained. Kevin had a huge personality, and his death affected so many.

Another sister, Marcia, sadly remembers how in a split-second, life changed for a very attractive Marilyn Carter when she was severely burned. It was an otherwise beautiful 4th of July day, but a gasoline-soaked rag which was set on fire to be celebratory was accidentally thrown at Marilyn when she was in a hammock. For Marcia and most of her friends, life would be relatively carefree and filled with the events that mark one's teenage years but for Marilyn, life would be filled with hospitalizations, surgeries, and pain. Such a heart-breaking disparity.

The one tragedy that affected my sister, Dee Dee, and the entire community, the most, was the loss of three high school senior boys on the water in the spring of 1961.

Dee Dee recalls that it was a warm sunny April 12, 1961 and her classmates Owen Bradford, Steven Stein, Gary McColgan, and Freddie Firestone had just enjoyed a vigorous after-school tennis practice. It was such a delightful spring day and the boys discussed going for a quick ride on Gary's 14' boat crossing the Great South Bay to Gilgo and back home. Gary lived towards Massapequa, on the water, and Dee believes they had all just taken a "safe boating course." Although Freddie wanted to go for the boat ride, he had a dentist appointment and begged off.

The day was so beautiful that none of the boys considered that the weather would change so drastically, but the ferocious spring Nor'easter came up quickly. The boys possibly could have thought to take shelter in one of the beach houses, but the boys were not law-breakers so that option would have seemed untenable, to break into someone else's home. Whether the outboard motor stopped working or the little boat was just no match for the wind is unknown as they tried to cross back over the Great South Bay, but what was known was that by early evening the boys had not returned home. The boys would have assuredly become disoriented in the stormy conditions and the Robert Moses Causeway lights wouldn't go on until the following month. If they had been able to see the lights, they possibly would have realized that they could have climbed out of the boat and walked through the waist-deep waters to the causeway but, only seeing darkness around them, it would have seemed that their best chance for safety and to avoid drowning was to stay with the boat. Due to the extreme weather conditions, however, they all died of exposure.

The tragedy is not forgotten by anyone in Dee's class. Even though it was a long time ago, in some ways, it seems like only yesterday. It is always discussed when any of the classmates occasionally meet. For some, it was not just a personal loss, but a loss to the world and to faith in anything other than chaos.

Owen's father worked at Republic Aviation, as did our dad. He called our dad around midnight to see if our boat was in the water so that we could do a water search but it was not, nor after numerous phone calls by Dad did anyone we know have their boat in the water yet. However, as soon as dawn came with its teeming rain and wind, we went out by car to scan all the waterways from the perspective of the roads. As Dad drove near Zachs Bay at Jones Beach, Dee remembers asking him to stop because she "had a feeling about that location," but with the Nor'easter still severe, we couldn't see anything and we kept driving. Needless to say, Dee always regrets that she had not been more insistent to look in that area, even though the driving rain precluded seeing very far. Nevertheless she still is left with that nagging regret… maybe if it could possibly have helped.

Freddie Firestone, who missed the boat ride, moved up to the position of class valedictorian. He had been third in the class prior to the accident but the boys who were the original valedictorian and salutatorian both died in the boat. Freddie left for Cornell that fall and was never the same.

Dee recalls:

> We were all in the same classroom 'A' track; though the four of them were the real A's. Owen had 800 on both his SATs and was accepted at MIT. Aside from being angelic, he was the nicest and president of the class. He used to sit next to me at lunch and fly through his math homework since he had been studying Greek and Latin at home in the evening. Steve was going to be my prom date. All the boys were wonderful, but Owen was beyond. I think of them often…not every day but almost.

> I do remember going to Steve Stein's house to visit the family and I remember when they made the announcement of finding the bodies over the loudspeaker at school. We all went to our homerooms (mine was where they would have been). Mrs. Koop, our teacher, left im-

mediately. Who wouldn't? Yet, I had the feeling...What about us?

I remember being in the car with my dad the next morning at daybreak, and looking at the bay from the end of Clocks Boulevard in E. Massapequa. The storm had come up suddenly and was a strong Nor'easter with temps dropping into the 30s. The Fire Island Coast Guard won't go beyond the Amity Cut and the Jones Beach Coast Guard boat capsized. Later that day, I had a class trip (eighth grade) to see a play in NYC, and Gracie Bradford (younger sister of Owen) was in my class. I recall seeing the headlines in papers of the tragedy in newsstands when we exited the theater, and the entire class blocking this so Gracie wouldn't see it.

Gracie's parents met her at the Amityville train station. I remember that Mr. Bradford had asked my dad if he had any connections at Republic for a helicopter but the weather was too ferocious for it in the early dawn hours. Later, I found out that an old bayman, Pat Abernathy, had calculated where they should be, given the wind and currents. He and a helicopter met at about 11 a.m., only to find two of the boys already deceased and one who died very soon thereafter.

Apparently, the boys had engine troubles, started floating southwest towards the Jones Inlet (sort of), threw the anchor and couldn't see land because of no lights. Due to the high tide, they floated over an island outside of Zachs Bay, but the anchor finally caught—a few hundred yards further they would have ended up on the causeway land. This tragedy was such big news that it was even listed as far away as in the *Utica Observer*. It's a story of Amityville and the Great South Bay that I've never forgotten in my entire life here.

After sixty years, a scholarship in the boys' names is still awarded yearly.

MEMORIES BY THE SEASON

by Dorothy Garvin

Our family moved to Amityville from Brooklyn, NY, in 1956. We were part of a migration from the city to the suburbs. I still live in the ranch-type home that my parents purchased in 1956, on Swartout Place, near the canals. I graduated from Amityville Memorial High School in 1959, attended Molloy College, and returned to Amityville as a Social Studies teacher, teaching grades 7–12 for 36 years. I am happily enjoying retirement now!

Let me try to retrieve some memories of growing up in Amityville. There are so many happy events to recall. I'll pick some of my favorites from the seasons of the year.

Autumn...The ragamuffin parade and the smiling face of Chief William Kay. Walking to the high school with my sister, Ronnie, along Ocean Ave. in brand new shoes and returning in the afternoon, barefoot, because of the blisters that occurred! The thrilling football games...number 31, Bernie Wyatt, coach Lou Howard, and the Warrior team that was famous for its winning seasons!

Winter...Oh the great times we spent ice skating on the very bumpy frozen canal near our home. The excitement of seeing the Great South Bay frozen and ice skating from the Village Dock at the end of Richmond Avenue...even watching small Volkswagens drive across the Bay!

Spring/Summer...Watching the arrival of the horseshoe crabs from the Richmond Ave. dock, on the night of the June full moon...what a sight to see and hear; these prehistoric creatures that were, and still are, used for bait!

And who could forget the beautiful 4th of July Parade? I even remember seeing a very aged veteran from World War I or the Civil War. Oh, the talented Black marching band strutting down Broadway...the floats...so many people attending. Swimming to the floating dock at the Amityville Beach and thinking that you had swum a mile! Then at night watching the magnificent fireworks from the foot of Richmond Avenue.

AMITYVILLE, A VILLAGE OF FRIENDS THAT MADE ME WHAT I AM...

by Jimmy McNabb

It was late autumn, 1961, when, for a rather long list of circumstances, I found myself sitting in a sophomore English class filled with strangers, all of whom seemed pleasant but, noticeably, not a bit curious about this new person in their midst. More to my point, not as interested in finding out about me as I was in finding out about them. I so much wanted a connection, a pal, a friend. I wanted to attach a history to everyone I was sitting with, to know more about them, who they were? Who were the sports guys, who were the serious scholars, who were both, who were the class wits and, most importantly, who would become a friend?

The class was led with precision by Sally Wallenstein, the teacher with shockingly red hair who I am certain at one point in her life had a yellow convertible. I was also sure that Ms. Wallenstein was a tea drinker, not coffee, strictly tea, probably English Breakfast with just a dash of milk. It was that moment that I realized I was even trying to attach a life history to the teachers and staff in a desperate attempt to form a connection to these strangers. A history that was a bit longer than the one-day history I shared with this new community.

Well, the point is, this redheaded tea drinker was an enormous help to me with this process of friend-making. Ms. Wallenstein was the first to introduce me to another person in Amityville. The introduction would become one of the more meaningful introductions of my young life. The significance of this first introduction can only be described as fortunate, extremely fortunate for me, as the introduction was to Carol Nehring, a treasured friend to this day.

That first day was a bit stressful, but Carol made it easier and made me a lot more comfortable with her brief welcome speech from the front of the class. Little did I know, at that moment, that three years on Carol and I would go to the Senior Prom together after sharing many happy experiences during high school. I would get to know and respect Carol as well as her entire family who were so welcoming to me. We spent a fair amount of time together, sailing on her dad's magnificent sailboat, working on class activities together and even competing against each other sailing at the Narrasketuck Yacht Club; all fun times with great memories throughout our high school years and beyond.

The relationship between Carol and me was a very natural one that developed over time, providing me with some wonderful memories and continued to produce ongoing experiences beyond high school. At one point I found myself living next door to Carol's kid sister, Janet, after moving back after several years in London.

I also got to be great pals with Carol's slightly older sister, Ginger. We became good friends as we worked across the street from each other in New York City on Park Avenue at 47th Street. Ginger worked for one of the executives at Chemical Bank while I was a Senior Trainee at a British company. One of my most fond memories of Ginger was that she generally and generously lent me about ten dollars most Thursdays as a bridge loan to my payday. Trainees do not make a large salary, even Executive Trainees. Ginger did work at a Bank and that is what banks do!

So, it seems that the very first person I was introduced to in Amityville set the tone for the friendships I was fortunate enough to form in this strange, but wonderful little village. The village that I came to know, soon adopt, and eventually love.

Amityville was different when compared to where I came from; new to me were canals and creeks, the Great South Bay, boats, natural space, open fields, lawns and gardens, some with pools, small streets, stop signs rather than traffic lights, ball fields, sports bleachers, tennis courts and the sense of a village, all quite different indeed, welcoming but different.

Adding to my mystery was this slight, subtle distance that my new classmates seemed to maintain those early days. Everyone seemed open enough, friendly enough as indicated by the warm smiles and simple eyewinks indicating a sign of hello or welcome, but not quite a full embrace. I wondered if I would ever find a good pal or make a true friend. I felt I didn't bring a lot of commonality with me to my new village and my new acquaintances; I couldn't sail, I wasn't great with sports, I didn't grow up here or even nearby, compounded by the fact that where I was now living in Amityville didn't really come with a nearby neighbor, not one. I soon realized I was not in the part of town where it would be easy to find people to pal around with, which so often leads to friendship.

As a few days became a few weeks, it seemed to me that this sense of hold-back or reluctance to reach out on the part of my classmates was, in a strange way, a form of honesty, a natural reaction not to impose oneself. If they were to step forward, these future friends would need a reason, a circumstance or incident to bring us together. What did we have in common, a place where a simpler association could be seeded, perhaps a hobby, a sport, even at church? It did not seem there were many opportunities open to me.

Up to this point I could not understand why no one seemed to take the step. In other words, I placed the blame on my new classmates, I held them totally responsible for my dilemma. Then, in a moment of clarity, I realized that I shared at least half the burden of reaching out, maybe even more than half. Perhaps the step forward should come from me. FLASH! I suddenly realized that it may be me creating the sense of distance. From that moment, I vowed to myself that I would take the steps to do my best to be the one to break the distance, to make a difference and reach out myself. Now, I just needed to figure out how.

Gym class or lunchtimes seemed to provide great opportunities for reaching out and I set out to do just that; I did my best and it seemed to help. I found that once an actual conversation occurred, more by circumstance than initiative, those winks and smiles became words actually spoken: "good morning" or "how are you doing?" even the occasional, "good to see you, Jim." It seemed a slow progress to an impatient guy like me, but it was now happening and was proven, without doubt, to be well worth the wait. I was beginning to consider myself a member of our new community.

As I gradually became more comfortable with Amityville, Amityville seemed to become more comfortable with me and this new relationship provided me with newly increased enthusiasm about myself and my future. This was a new and different beginning, a beginning where I could determine my life's course, as captain not passenger. I found I was sharing times with people whom I liked and even admired. Classmates that followed directions and parent's wishes and rules because they agreed with those rules and wishes, not just because they were being forced to follow them for fear of retribution or punishment. This was all new to me, to be with kids like this, kids that assumed self-responsibility, kids that knew what they wanted, kids who were comfortable with themselves, kids that understood study and hard work would lead to a better future. I had not shared time with kids like that ever before. These young people just assumed they would go to college and, by extension, just knew they would have an interesting and meaningful career. This down-to-earth attitude made such assumptions even more real and believable. I grew to embrace some of these attitudes myself, realizing these feelings were good for me as well. Amityville was becoming promising; this was a change that I was beginning to embrace and I saw it as good for me as well. I remain profoundly grateful to this day for these lessons—lessons learned from friends and classmates as much as teachers—and they have stood me well to this day.

I also thought back to that first day that introduced me to yet another eye-opening experience. At the end of that first day, as the bell rang ending the last class, I stood up and watched everyone march out of the room in a most orderly and mature manner. I headed down the front staircase, and out the front doors of the school facing Merrick Road. To my surprise there was not one school bus as I had expected to find. After building up the courage to ask a total stranger where the buses for North Amityville would be, she looked at me questioningly replying, "North Amityville?". (As it happened my family ran a business in North Amityville, and they chose for us to live there as well). After a pause, I inhaled her directions, quietly thanked her, and headed in the opposite direction.

This tiny exchange proved to be another first on this my first day; the social structure of an integrated school which I had never experienced before. I have grown to be so grateful for this experience. It changed me and, in many ways, shaped much of who I am today. It took a few minutes to navigate the corridors, few they may be but new to me. I found my way out what seemed to be the back of the building past the gym. Finally, I made my way to the precise bus I was meant to take. Stepping up into the bus, I turned left and walked toward the back with my eyes focused straight ahead until I came to an empty row with no neighbor. Shortly after throwing my jacket and books on the overhead rack, I collapsed in my seat. I surveyed the folks on the bus to suddenly realize I was the only non-black person on that bus. Wow, I thought to myself, this is different. I have never had an experience like this, what should I do, where should I look, should I talk with someone, could I make up a question to break the silence? I did not want to be overly friendly for fear of seeming patronizing, but I also did not want to seem aloof for obvious reasons.

My head was spinning. I swallowed as I thought to myself, I am experiencing something that my black classmates experience almost every day in the America of the early '60s. I suddenly found myself asking what seemed to be a hundred questions, all at the same time. I was not quite sure how to process this experience and, again, not sure where to look and not appear to be staring, I stood up grabbed a book from the overhead rack and pretended to read. But I could not read, too many devils dancing around in my young head. I did have a hundred questions and could not wait to get home to share these questions and hopefully get some suggestions from my parents. What is expected of me? I am not really a part of my neighbor's tribe in North Amityville but I'm equally not really part of Carol's tribe either. How will I handle this, who now will I become pals with? Which group will accept me, who will like me in this new world? Will my new neighborhood citizens resent me for intruding on their bus? Would they just accept me as a neighbor? I began to try to work out how I would be making my way through this new world. When you are 14 or 15 a new school is your world, and I was exploring it without a compass. On the bus, no one really seemed to take note of my presence, not glad to see me or bothered by my being there. There was one minor exception, two attractive girls slightly paused as they passed my row, they glanced with wide eyes, smiled just short of laughter, and openly giggled as they took their seats. I believe they were saying something like, "New kid's not so bright…he's on the wrong bus."

My parents were a bit puzzled by my questions and I think feared that I might be slightly prejudiced. It seemed crazy to me but I found myself defending my position rather than getting the advice I was looking for that night. My mother concluded this little chapter of our dinner conversation with a succinct; "Just be yourself Jimmy, hopefully you will make friends with those kids that share your interests, just try to get along with everyone. There are more similarities than differences, now eat."

I went to bed that night really looking forward to the next day and my new world. I imagined and almost practiced how I would greet my new neighbors on the bus in the morning but fell off to sleep almost immediately with lots of questions in my head, all rich material for my dreams.

The next morning, as I waited for the bus, I was still running through my lines and gestures of greeting. When it finally arrived, I simply got on the bus, returning a few smiles as I walked down the aisle to find a seat. The routine was set and that is how it carried on for the next three years. No script or rehearsed lines needed or employed.

This remarkable growing experience continued for all three years with tutoring and guidance from classmates and friends. One of those friends was a celestial creature named Cele Husing. Cele was inspiring to me, leading her life by her own standards, extremely high standards at that, but most importantly, unique to Cele. Cele introduced me to her friend with whom she enjoyed an interracial friendship and relationship. Cele introduced me to Billy Garran without flare, as though there was nothing to notice. This relationship and opinions about it opened my eyes to so many issues, so many questions and taught me volumes. I am deeply grateful to both of them and adore Cele to this day. It should not have been an issue, I sensed that to my core, but there it was, and it was an issue. I was so fortunate to get to know and love these two incredibly special people. We are still struggling to this day to define a democracy by the way we live our lives. That is how it happens it seems to me, the way we conduct our own behavior and attitudes shape the world in which we live. I learned this in Amityville. I am hopeful that this recent election may help to speed up the process of the healing we all deserve.

What I learned about honesty, life, fairness, prejudice, acceptance, understanding, empathy, kindness, misunderstandings and needless disrespect has been, for the most part, learned in Amityville. Lessons that I hold dear now. I remain extremely grateful to Amityville and the people I met there, that I became friends with and have grown to love.

Having said that, I was still living in North Amityville which I sort of viewed as an obstacle to my social life and to potential friendships, but it, too, was providing me with another life-learning opportunity. I had the chance to witness firsthand that my theory of just assuming college was a part of your life did not work for everyone. Not all my new classmates could assume a college education, or that a career of their dreams would be a part of their futures. It was a daunting discovery—it seemed so unfair, but it was selfishly for me, a rich opportunity to be exposed to this juxtaposed experience at the age of 15. This was truly a vivid experience for me, and I have carried the influence it had on me every day since that first autumn day in 1961. It opened my eyes to the reality of life, its opportunities, drawbacks, and its sad misunderstanding and ugly prejudice. My new experiences in Amityville taught me to respect life, all life and to try to make a more well-balanced life which I strive for to this very day.

Coming from a school that was remarkable in its indifference to people, to a place where everyone seemed to matter was, in so many ways, a surprise to me. I thought I would have a difficult time adjusting to this new place and new kids—I was wrong. My new classmates seemed more normal to me every day, missing that pretense I had grown accustomed to where I came from. Girls without makeup and the supposedly chic black clothing and living style as a personality; real or not. The girls in my new town did not use much, if any, makeup, tease their hair, wear black, have frighteningly long fingernails; they appeared more normal or natural which to me translated to being more confident, more honest about themselves and more open to the world. The guys were pretty much the same, dressing for themselves not as a competition or display of hipness, just one's own clothes—sort of, what you saw was what you got. Kids were not pronounced popular or unpopular, just Becky, or Chris, or Chip, Pete, or Billy. We all seemed to find something in each other and that helped me be able to enjoy something about all the people that I have met in my life.

As the days went by I became friendly with some people in my new world but discovered that geography played a role in the development of new relationships. In the early '60s we were an integrated school but not necessarily an interrelated or integrated town. I did find that I had more in common with the students who came from the south end of town. This confused me a bit as I lived in a totally different world but now no one seemed to notice or care. I loved this feeling, there was definite separation but it was for the most part not based on judgements as it was on geography, which plays a very big role in one's life without a driver's license.

I was never a great sportsman, but I like sports, games that required passing or catching of balls was a task for me as I am legally blind since birth in my left eye. I felt I needed to get involved in sport to create some common interest and ground with my new friends. This allowed me to meet some terrific people, some of whom I am still in touch with all these years later. Two of these friends are William Powell and Peter Hudson, formerly Bill, and Pete.

Pete, in those days, was a close buddy and we spent a lot of time together despite the geography dilemma; it was mostly spent at his house on Richmond Avenue. Pete was the one who taught me how to sail, or as best he could, given his student. Pete's family became a second family. His mom was a special person, so kind and warm to me. Pete's slightly older sister, Barbara, was a great character and tease...I had a young kid's crush on Barb and was sorry when she left for Keuka College and I would not be able to share time with both Peter and Barb. Peter's older sister, Judy, was a great person as well and she fascinated me. While she was further separated from Pete and me by age, she was a person I truly admired for having her own mind and marching beautifully to her very own drum. I genuinely cared for this family as I did with the Powells, the Murtaghs, the Irelands, the Nehrings and several more that so willingly embraced me and made me feel so very welcome.

Amityville and its people will also remain a huge part of my life and a part that I am so thankful for as I think back to those remarkable days.

Billy Powell and I have stayed in touch sporadically but firmly since high school. Billy is a solid guy with a great family. Our friendship is based on Billy's wondrous skills of teasing. As I mentioned, we became good friends on the soccer team, even though I was not quite first string! I recall one away game with the team. When we were on the bus headed back to Amityville, Coach Schmidt called out from the front of the bus, "Anyone have any injuries to report?" Without a minute's delay, Billy Powell shouted out, "Yes, McNabb does, he's got splinters from the bench!" Of course, the bus broke into laughter as I was trying to come up with a plan for Billy to be in need of his family's services at Powell's Funeral Home.

These Amityville friendships have lasted the test of time and have been so supportive to me at difficult moments in my life, living on my own for the most part. These incredibly special people have provided me with remarkable and major comfort and strength as well as a sense of family. The amount of support I have known, I will never forget.

When I was able to drive, I would visit the Powell family in the evening until Billy's dad would ask in a gruff voice, "Have you finished all your lessons, Jimmy?" Which was my invitation to take my leave. There was a time where going to college was at risk due to family issues and it was Billy's sister, Janet, who sat me down in their sunroom one afternoon and totally convinced me to change course and go to college, which I did.

Thanks to the wonderful 50th Class Reunion, conceived, planned, and produced by Carol Nehring with Sandee Ketcham Molden, we were all brought back together to share a remarkable weekend. I was thrilled to be reunited with so many dear friends with whom I now am speaking on a regular basis. Several of whom I have grown to know so much better and to really appreciate. Tom Glum and his wife Anne are key among those friends that include Sandee, Carol, Pete, Billy, Tommy O'Neill, and his charming wife Carol and of course Cele.

The move to Amityville has proven to be a life-changing event for me; fostering a change in me; a broadened threshold of understanding, acceptance, and open-mindedness. These are the people who have become essential in my life and provided me with an experience of amity, not just a definition.

FAMILY STORIES

FAMILY STORIES

FAMILY STORIES

ESCAPE TO AMITYVILLE

by Virginia Synan Swartz

When I was seven and would lay in my bed in Dormitory Four at St. Dominic's Home for Children in Blauvelt, NY, planning my escape helped me to fall asleep. Escape was my only option to the prayers I said nightly with great faith and optimism. I prayed my parents would find a home for us, because in the summer of 1947 we were homeless. It was why we were now at St. Dominic's Home.

Then, hallelujah! When I was eleven, those prayers were finally answered. On the last day of the school year in 1951, we were told we were going home in two days. Two days! This was surely a good thing, because no matter how I planned, my escape route always included a trek through Bear Mountain, where I was sure there actually were bears, and I was afraid one might even try to eat me.

I could not have been more joyful to hear we were going home. My father got a job at St. Martin of Tours in Amityville, Long Island, New York, as both the sexton of the church and the janitor of the school, and miracle of miracles, a house came with the job!!! We would have a home of our own. Finally.

And, it wasn't just any old house, either. This one had been the former convent for the nuns, the Amityville Dominicans, which is either ironic or serendipitous, since we were ruled by the Blauvelt Dominicans at The Home. The house also had a chapel where the good sisters could follow all their daily mass and prayer routines. Can you imagine? We called it the Cold Room because it had no heat. It did have an elevated platform at one end of the room where the altar must have been located, and though there was no railing, it's probably a safe assumption.

The house was magnificent, for many reasons. It had both a front porch and an attic. It was located right on Oak Street, which was the east/west main street, and not far from Broadway which went north and south. It had a lovely backyard with a gate that backed up to St. Martin's schoolyard.

So, many days I would sit on the front porch and just watch the cars go by. And I'd watch the people, too, making up stories about them in the bubble above my head, as they went by. Everyday, a man, I believe his name was Angelo Camarota, would walk up Oak Street to Broadway. I think he may have had polio (this was pre-polio vaccine days and he may have been left with a physical handicap). He had a lovely smile and would always share it with me along with a big, friendly wave. Someone I didn't know was waving to me. Smiling. Helping me to feel welcome in my new home and my new village. Amityville, even then, was called The Friendly Village.

The attic in the house was a true treasure, where I found all sorts of goodies and leftovers, from boxes of clothing, to pieces of furniture, large and small, and all manner of bric-a-brac treasures, left there by whom, I would wonder. It didn't matter for it was all fodder for my imagination to run wild. Oh, the stories I could make up, and the mysteries I would find in every darkened corner.

The real joy, however, in those first days home from St. Dominic's in the summer of 1951, was everyday life in Amityville. At St. Dominic's my world was limited to The Plot, the dormitory, and the refectory; now my world was limited to just the little village from the railroad tracks to the Post Office located on Broadway about a block or so beyond Avon Place and the A&P. The schoolyard, of course, had its own charms and intrigues...and the church...Oh My Goodness! Once, when my father was ringing the bells for the Angelus at noon, he let me hold the rope... which almost took me right into the bell tower!

Growing Up in Amityville

As it happened, we arrived in Amityville at the start of St. Martin's Annual Bazaar, which was set up in the schoolyard. All I had to do was go out our back gate and I was in the middle of this great adventure. There were rides and music and hundreds of people taking chances on the many different game booths; and, there was every variety of food being sold at various booths throughout the bazaar. It was at night, so it was lit up very brightly, adding to the excitement. Everywhere I went people would say hello, as though they knew me, though I had no idea who they were. They were friendly, and laughing, and excited, and having a grand time. What a way to start the summer, but even better, what a way to start my new life!

St. Dominic's Home was a good place for my sibs and me to be when we lived there. Though it served its purpose, it was a bit like being in jail, and God was the warden. Because the nuns were kind, but strict, our coming and going anywhere at whim was certainly never allowed. At The Home, walking in lines, two by two, and no talking were the everyday rules, except during the time on the playground, aka The Plot. So, now, here we were at 19 Oak Street, with the door wide open and the freedom to come and go without having to ask permission, whenever I wanted; it took some getting used to.

But, when Christopher's Stationery Store is waiting with the newspapers, both morning and afternoon editions, and when Lomot's and Johnson's were waiting with every variety of fresh veggies, fruits, and groceries, as well as delicious meats, and The Bakery next door to Lomot's, with the most scrumptious selection of fresh made buns, was on the list, who wouldn't want to walk up to the village whenever the request was made?

If it wasn't Lomot's and Johnson's, it was Bohack's across the street when it was still on Broadway, or Fisher's Ice Cream Parlor…where they made their own whipped cream! And Phanemiller's Pharmacy, or the Post Office, where my father would often send me to pick up the rectory mail…and how exciting it was to be entrusted with the combination to the postal mailbox! Leibang's Hardware Store was always a mystery to me, but fun to browse; and, there was McClellan's Department store where I bought my own curlers and my first lipstick; Lang's Shoe Store, where I picked out my own first pair of shoes, not given to me from the donated clothes to The Home, were also part of my daily adventures. The shoes were very soft flats and were two toned with the toe top one color and the rest of the shoe a different color, neither of which I remember. It was the two tones that intrigued me. My favorite all time clothing stores, before Martin's Department Store came to Babylon, were Shim's and Lowy's. I bought socks and underwear in Shim's, and my first pair of Dungarees in Lowy's, and, I picked them out all by myself!

There were many kind people in my life in that summer of 1951. The Galloway family for example—Jack, Francis, Patty and Joanne. Mr. Galloway worked for St. Martins, and often they would invite us to watch their television in the evening, a very big deal kindness in those days. They also took us with them to see the synchronized swimming shows at the Jones Beach Pool, which was at night, and quite dazzling. Until then, I had never seen anything like these spectacular performances. Is it too late, I sometimes wonder, to thank them for their generosity? Because, if I never have done so in person, I have many times in that bubble above my head.

Most of all, in the Summer of 1951, there was Katherine Coletto. Her mom and mine had become friends before we had come home from St. Dominic's, and lucky for me, she was probably encouraged to be nice to me…because she was really, really nice, and I had a new best friend. Somebody who wasn't family liked me, and made plans to do things with me…like go to the movies every Saturday, or teach me to fish in Avon Lake, or go to the wonderland of the library, where she introduced me to this very funny game.

The game went like this: as we went through the stacks, we would pick up a book, read the title, then add, "under the covers." For example, "The Thurber Carnival… under the covers," or "Norman Vincent Peale's Guide to Confident Living…under the covers," or, "The Adventures of Tom Sawyer…under the covers." Then we would laugh ourselves silly and run out of the library, before we got into trouble. To this day, I have wonderful memories of time spent with Katherine and her very large, very loud, and very happy Coletto family. I'm also happy to say we are still in touch, as well.

As the years went on, many wonderful, and some not so wonderful, events filled my every waking moment, but it was the summer of 1951, the people, the village, and all I discovered in my new home that has helped to form who I am today. So, yes, I never had to go through with my escape plan, my prayers were answered many times over. I realize how blessed, and lucky I am, to have lived in The Friendly Village. Today, I live in another state, and am very happy here, but whenever people ask me where I'm from, I always say Amityville. It's where my heart still lives.

FAMILY STORIES

MY AMITYVILLE STORY

by José Creamer

The ads appeared in several New York City newspapers. It was the late 1910s and Amityville was being advertised as a place where New Yorkers could find respite from city life in a bucolic beach community in Suffolk County. Surely my grandfather saw these ads, most likely in the *Brooklyn Eagle*, because Amityville was the place he chose to make a new life for himself and his family.

My grandfather, Francis A. Creamer, was born in Maryland, but came to New York while serving in the U.S. Army, and never left. He joined the newly formed New York City Police Department after being discharged from the army. His appointment was signed by Police Commissioner Theodore Roosevelt.

Mr. Creamer married Mary Farrell and raised two children, Frank and Alice. After Mary passed away in 1904, my grandfather married Ida Humphreys and they moved to Park Slope in Brooklyn. Francis and Ida had five sons, and along the way my grandfather attained the rank of captain. Captain Creamer retired from the police force in 1917, and a few years later, he made the move to his retirement dream– Amityville.

My grandparents and their four sons (their firstborn died of polio) set up house at 56 Dixon Ave., just across from the former Brunswick Hospital. There, my father Richard and his brothers Charles, William and James, grew up and attended the local schools. I'm not sure where my father attended elementary school, but I know he played football for Amityville High School, and later attended Georgia Tech.

My father's oldest brother Charles (we called him Uncle Chubb, although he wasn't chubby) married Elna Egelund, who was the daughter of Oscar Egelund, a longtime Amityville resident. They moved into 38 Dixon Ave. Along the way, my uncle Bill and my father met the sisters Ramona and Rosa Pérez, who lived in a stone house on North Broadway. My father was at Georgia Tech, William at NYU and James at Amityville High School, when their father passed away in 1938.

My mom and dad married in 1940, just before the U.S. entered the war. My oldest brother and sister were born amid the preparation for war and shortly thereafter my dad joined the Navy and was assigned to a destroyer escort in the North Atlantic. After the war my father returned to Amityville and the family moved into 38 Dixon Ave. After I and my older sister were born, the family moved into 56 Dixon Ave. (my grandmother Ida passed away before I was born). Soon, two more sisters were born, and it was time to find a bigger home. Some new houses were being built near the high school and my parents bought a lot, hired a builder, and our new house on Wood Ave. was ready. A younger brother and sister joined the family soon after and we definitely had a "full house."

It was 1955 and life was good in the Village. Wood Ave. and the streets around it were not main thoroughfares, so walking or biking was never a problem for young kids. My best friend, Billy Brennan, lived around the corner from me and we had other kids to play with all around the neighborhood. As with most other kids who grew up during this era, life was much different than it is today. If we weren't in school, we were off on our bikes, leaving our houses in the morning and staying out until it was time for dinner. We didn't have any restrictions, but we knew enough to ask permission if we wanted to go farther afield than normal. I remember going to a Yankees game with my oldest sister when I was eight years old and she was 14. We took the Long Island Railroad into Manhattan and switched to the IRT subway line to the stadium in the Bronx and returned. To this day I can't believe that one, we went to the Bronx alone and two, that our parents let us!

We played stickball in the streets (my oldest sister taught me to throw and catch), flew kites on the football field at the high school, fished at Avon Lake and walked to the beach to swim. We biked to a burger place on Merrick Road (could it be Burger King?), where 10 cents bought you an ice cream cone with sprinkles. We used to try to fish out coins from the storm drains using bubble gum on the end of a stick. How those coins got in the drain in the first place is a mystery. If anything happened to us, Dr. Bradley, whose office was around the corner, was always available to heal us. He was our own urgent care facility.

In addition to friends, we were fortunate to have many of our relatives close by. My mother's mother and brother moved into a house three doors down on Wood Ave. My Uncle Bill and Aunt Ramona moved back to the town with their three children after living in South America for several years, and though it was a little bit of a hike to their house, we did it often. They lived on Coles Ave. and the canal at the end of the street was a great place to go crabbing. They had a great finished basement that was always cool, even on the hottest days of the summer (most houses did not have air conditioning).

My Uncle Chubb and Aunt Elna lived on South Bayview Ave. and owned and operated a deli (known as the Corner Store) on North Broadway, that was originally owned by Elna's father, Oscar Egelund. It was always a great treat to drive to the store with my father to buy things, because my Uncle Chubb would always give us a Charms lollipop, which back then was large and lasted a long time. Uncle Chubb and Aunt Elna's daughter, Barbara, lived on Union Place, just up the street from St. Martin School, which all of my siblings and I attended. She was married to Pat Pescitelli and I remember them as being two of the nicest people I ever knew.

My Uncle Jim and Aunt Marge (who both attended Amityville High) had left Amityville and moved to Islip along with their three children. They visited us often and I remember that no matter what day it was, Aunt Marge was always completely put together, dressed as if she was about to head out to a garden party. She always reminded me of Donna Reed from the Donna Reed Show! Frank Creamer and Alice Creamer Boylan (my father's step-siblings) also lived in Amityville, as did George and Mattie Velsor Humphreys, my father's grandparents, and Anna Humphreys Hyland, my father's aunt.

In the fall of 1956, I started school at St. Martin. My first teacher was Sister Marie Germain. She was the best teacher I ever had (and I think she kind of liked me, too!). My cousin Carmen joined me in that class, which was fun, especially because we had the same last name and people thought we were twins. On to second, third and then to fourth grade, where we had Mrs. Busking, another great teacher. She seated us according to how well we did in class. The kids with the good grades sat in the back row, the number one student seated in the left rear corner. It seemed that Maureen Howard always held that spot, challenged by Jane Howley and Jane Chadwick. I was in the running, but because I was lazy, I never made it past the fourth best seat.

Our class stayed together, at least through the fourth grade. I remember Susie Walker, James Gary, Michael Hoy, Michael Whalen, Michael McDonough (lots of Michaels then), James McDonough, James Darcey, Patty Pollock, Nancy Stewart, Donald Murphy, Nancy Hill, the Joseph twins, Joan (my first love) and Jean, Kevin White, John Cheviot and so many more I cannot remember. They were all good kids, and although we had our differences from time to time, I don't remember anyone being bullied or kids being treated unkindly (other than Michael Hoy, who got into it with an upperclassman and had to go to the hospital with a bleeding head wound). We were all trying to deal with the Civil Defense drills (in case of nuclear attack, hide under your desk!), the Cold War, and impending puberty.

Towards the end of fourth grade, I got the news that my Dad's company was moving to Connecticut from New York. Goodbye Joan, and Billy. Goodbye Wood Ave., Avon Lake, St. Martin Church, McClellan's, the German bakery, St. Martin School, Ms. Duryea (my swimming instructor), and Dr. Bradley. Goodbye to all those great times and great people. I miss you all still.

FAMILY STORIES

ILSE FALKENBACH KLEIN'S MEMORIES

As recounted by Susan Falkenbach Welch

In 2010, I asked my then-92-year-old Aunt Ilse to write some of her memories of growing up. With the older brothers all gone and my father Hans's death in September 2002, Ilse was the only one who could tell our family some of what it was like growing up in Amityville. The youngest, my Aunt Rosemarie, was six years younger and really did not have the same memories. Ilse sent me some hand-written notes and then some more soon after. She told me "spelling doesn't count!" I put them together, typed them up, and then sent her a copy and got her approval. In a few cases, I knew from records that a small detail had to be corrected. In many cases, I have much more information than she remembered, as well as provenance, such as NYS or USA census data about who lived in the household and where exactly the family lived. Mostly, though, they just confirmed what she remembered anyway. When the family moved to Amityville in 1923, Ilse and my dad were not yet 5 and 7. The older boys were 11, 13, and 14. Carl, Wolfie, and my dad all lived and worked in Amityville for decades longer, until they retired. Wolfie raised two sons in Amityville, Carl and Drew; and my father and mother raised my sister Carol and me in Amityville through those same years. Ilse moved to Huntington when she married in 1939 and raised a family there, Ferdy moved to New Jersey sometime after serving in World War II, and Rosemarie and her family lived in Amityville for some of the years her children were growing up.

This is Ilse's Amityville story.

I was born in Bound Brook, New Jersey, on August 16, 1918, almost two years after my brother Hansie. I was the second child to be born in America and the first daughter after five boys. One baby boy had died from whooping cough in 1909 in Germany—he was just six months old. Mother and my brother Carl also had the disease, but they recovered.

In the years after they arrived here in America in 1912, and until after the first World War, my father and the family lived on private estates in New York State. Before I was born, one position was for three years on the Francis Lloyd Stetson estate called Skylands Farm in Sterlington, Rockland County, where my grandfather was a landscaper and caretaker. Another one was when he was a Superintendent on the J. C. Penney estate, White Haven, in White Plains, Westchester County, and the family lived in the caretaker's house. These positions, in which he had several others working under him, were held either before I was born or when I was very little so I don't really remember anything about them. I do recall that there are photos with large estates and some of us children are in those photos.

As the first daughter, I remember being "the apple of my father's eye." In 1922, the family traveled back to Germany to visit and lived there for several months. According to our passenger records from our return, not just Hansie and I who were born in the United States but all of the family were now U.S. citizens. At least one of the reasons that we returned to America was that inflation was so bad in Germany. According to family stories, when Father worked and was paid, he would bring a wheel barrow filled with money that day to buy whatever they needed—bread, shoes, or whatever, because the next day it would only cost more.

In February 1923, most of the family—Carl Otto, Kate, young Carl, Hansie, and I—returned to the United States. Wolfie and Ferdy did not return until November of that year. Father had placed them in a monastery boarding school for several months in Cochem, Germany, on the Moselle River. We must have had some means as we traveled in second class, not steerage. I remember that at first when we got back, we lived in a house on 112 Bayview Avenue in Amityville. In 1924, we moved to 41 South Railroad Avenue and I remember that there was no electricity in that house. In December 1924, Rosemarie was born, and the Ketcham family next door was very helpful. I remember having a live Christmas tree with real candles. We played at a soda place on Railroad Avenue and at a creamery, and there was a nearby pond known as Avon Lake. I also remember that I had diphtheria. My brothers were then given shots by the visiting nurse and they were angry about that.

Sometime in 1924 or early 1925, Father got a head injury from a falling tree limb while working on a job. He lingered for over a year and later died on December 13, 1926. He had been a Freemason, and the Freemasons wanted to take Hansie, me, and Rosemarie (10, eight, and two years old) to a home in Utica in upstate New York. When Father died, my brother Carl was 18, Wolf was 15, and Ferdy was 14. Mother said "No" to the offer—that she would try to keep the family together,—and that is what she did. I remember that Father's body was in a funeral home on Route 110 near Railroad Avenue in a time when bodies were usually held at home. Rosemarie remembers being told that he was buried on her second birthday, December 16, 1926. He was, and his grave is in Amityville Cemetery.

For a while, Mother ran the family gardening business with the help of Carl—Carl had already quit school to help run the business while father was unable to work. They hired men directly from Germany to help. In 1927, with money from Father's life insurance, she bought the house on 16 Morris Street between Richmond Avenue and Central Avenue. She still owned that house when she died 50 years later in April 1977, at age 92. The house was a bungalow style, it had no cellar, water was hand pumped in the kitchen, and there was an outhouse.

Eventually, the boys added a large room to the back of the house and an indoor bathroom; but that, too, was unheated. The house was raised, a cellar was dug, and an electric pump was added to supply water inside. There was a furnace with a register in the living room but no other heat. There were four unheated bedrooms, two up and two down. Large bags of wet wash went to a Farmingdale laundry to be hung out to dry in the back yard.

In 1927, Mother's brother, Uncle Adi, came to live with us. He had a large vegetable garden, a grape arbor, and berry bushes. The family owned the adjoining lot that went through to the next side street, Riverside Street, and they had a nursery on that property. Mother did the paperwork on the landscaping business, and Carl and Wolf ran it. The boys built a small building in the back yard and put six cots in it, and that is where the men from Germany slept. There was also a cold outdoor shower in a small house and an outhouse for these men only. The men got paid plus they got room and board, which meant my mother was preparing three meals a day for at least fourteen people—six men, one brother, herself, and six kids. The six men took lunch on the job; they each got a quart of iced tea and four sandwiches. The boys came home for lunch, and everyone came home for supper.

When I was still growing up at home, Uncle Adi would tell me I could go to the beach after I finished peeling or preparing whatever bushel baskets of produce he had; but when I was done with one, he seemed to have another for me to do. I remember that sometimes I never did get to the beach as he had promised! Uncle Adi was still there into the 1950s when the first of our children were young.

Mother kept the books and made out the bills. Many times, I went out on my bike to collect from customers. Mother never did learn to drive. Carl was teaching her in North Amityville at one point, and a drunken man fell into the car—Carl actually knew him. That was the end of her driving!

The boys had one and then two trucks. Carl also had a large open eight-person touring car called a Hupmobile. He would take us to Freeport, which was a bigger town than Amityville, for some shopping. I did a lot of grocery shopping on my bike as it had a large front basket. In the winter, the boys drove taxis or a school bus or even drove for funerals. They would bring me a flower sometimes. They also did any odd jobs around town. We ate the vegetables and fruits that we had canned in the summer.

Carl, Wolf, and Ferdy went only through the eighth grade because they had to work after Father was injured and then later died. Hansie, I, and Rosemarie all graduated from Amityville High School. I and then Rosemarie became registered nurses—our mother didn't want her girls to be without some way to earn a living. Mother was well-educated in the Ursuline Convent in Hamont, Alsace-Lorraine, a region in northeast France that in the late 1800s was a part of the German Empire. Mother's education was, I think, equal to some college, but she didn't learn skills like bookkeeping! Father had an education in Germany equal to what a Farmingdale Aggie graduate in those days would have.

Some other recollections that I have include growing up in a house with eight people and one bathroom! I also remember all eight of us in the living room listening to the radio—*The Lone Ranger* and other stories.

I also have some memories of my Amityville school friends. One was sometime in the late 1920s when Rosemarie was maybe four and I was maybe 10 years old, we were standing with my friend, Tillie (Helene Nehring), on a boat in back of a house on Central Avenue. There were large ice chunks in the canal. Out of the blue, Rosemarie pushed Tillie off the boat and said "big fish!" We had to walk a couple of blocks to our house, all wet and freezing. Another one was when I was about eleven or twelve and Rosemarie about five or six. I had to mind Rosemarie and take her with me to my friends' houses or wherever I went. There were two creeks off South Bayview Avenue, one shallow and one deep. I would leave her at the shallow one, with other families, and go to the deep one with my friends. I told her "if you tell mother, I will drown you." She never told. I always had a boy's bike with a cross bar, on which she rode. Years later, probably about 1945, Rosemarie was the nurse in the labor room at Brunswick Hospital with a friend of mine, Evelyn, whom we called "PeeWee." She was one of the Wanser twins. Evelyn opened her eyes in the recovery room, looked at Rosemarie, and told her, "Oh, Rosemarie, I'm so glad you didn't drown."

In 1932 or so, I came home later than I was supposed to and sat on the cellar door. Mother wanted me inside to punish me. I sat there about two hours, until she said she wouldn't. She was strong-willed, but so was I! She really needed me to help as I was the one who helped her prepare all that food for all those men—my brothers and the workers. Around that time, there was a small bridge at the end of Morris Street on Central Avenue. Hansie had a small sailboat, and the mast couldn't be put up until after going under the bridge. So I helped him knock down the bridge—public property. Our crime never got discovered!

In about 1933, we had very heavy snow and the roads were covered. Mother told Hansie and me that we had to go to school anyway. We walked in snow as high as my knees for about one mile to school. When we got there, only the janitors had come in. Then we had to walk back!

In the mid-1930s, I remember that my brother Carl had nice white shirts. I used to take one to wear with my school jacket. Then I'd launder it, put it back, and he never knew! He would have been very angry… In those same years, our neighbor's daughter got married at home. Wolfie could play the piano, and we had an old one so the men from both families carried the piano next door. It was a fun wedding with Wolfie playing—he played by ear. Also in the mid-1930s, there were eight people living in the family home, and six men in the bungalow out back who worked in landscaping with my brothers. In order to stay after school for sports,

I had to peel as many as 20 pounds of potatoes each evening for the next day. I remember sometimes at 10 p.m. still doing that!

In 1936, I started dating Bill Klein, the first boy that the family didn't already know as he was not from Amityville. When he came for me, there was a big family discussion in German! Two brothers said "Okay," and two said, "No." Mother finally said "Okay." All that discussion and tension must have been especially hard for Bill as he was an only child!

In 1938, I came home from a date very late. I slept on the living room couch to avoid going through Mother's room to the upstairs, and Mother was very upset and told me so. My brother Hansie swore to Mother that he had seen me there earlier. Since Hansie never ever lied, truly, that got me out of trouble. He really thought he had seen me and was mortified when I thanked him for covering for me!

Also in 1938, for my brother Carl's wedding, I drew a picture of a dress I wanted—for sure I was no designer. I sent it to Louise Johnson, who lived in Amityville with her parents and her niece Eleanor McAlester. She had a job as a seamstress in a clothing factory and also designed and sewed clothing on her own. She made the dress for me and it fit me exactly. By that time, we all knew her niece, Ellie, as she was dating my brother Hansie. In 1940, Aunt Lou also made Ellie's wedding dress as well as the dresses for me and Ellie's other bridesmaids.

Before Hansie and Ellie got married in June 1940, Hansie created an apartment on the house out of the downstairs back bedroom. I can remember being on the roof helping! It had a separate entrance at the back of the house, one bedroom, a living room, a kitchen with a very small eating area, and a small bathroom. Hansie and Ellie lived there for about a year when they were first married. When they moved out, Mother received some income from that apartment for years by renting it out. Eventually, she moved into it herself and continued to receive income by renting out the big house.

Even though, looking back, I know it must have been a hard life, I do not remember being unhappy. I always remember eating well, too. We were a noisy, happy family.

Ilse Falkenbach Klein

PEACE AND HARMONY

by Carla Miller-Camacho

I was born on the hottest day of the year in August 1955 in Lakeside Hospital, Copaigue, NY. The hospital is now a condominium complex, but back in the day it was the alternative to having a baby in Brunswick Hospital in Amityville, which is also no longer there. It is amazing how many businesses and other landmarks no longer exist in Amityville, and we could never have imagined what our town was going to turn into over the years.

I am the youngest child of five, whom my single mother was raising alone. I don't wish to get into the particulars of our family dynamic, but suffice it to say that with a Hispanic last name, but being African-American (by definition) it might explain what life was like for us back in the 1960s. Amityville seemed to be the ideal place to raise children, with its multiple elementary schools, great upper schools and churches, Boys and Girls Scout troops, dance classes, music classes and a multiple of other activities for children of all ages and backgrounds.

I didn't know that I was "Black" until many years later, because we never discussed race in our house; probably because my great-grandfather on my mother's side was an Irishman. So, by the time I had started Kindergarten I had to wear green on St. Patrick's Day whether I wanted to or not...it was just a "tradition" in our family. My mother also had many, many white friends in the neighborhood. And, one of my close friends was a little white girl who lived down the street. (Anna Reiners whose family was German.)

I grew up on a street not far from Rt. 110 (the main highway), named Coolidge Avenue and then we moved to a bigger house in another part of the town. Lou Howard was the town's mayor and his family lived right down the street. Our neighbors were a mix of practically all races and colors. Like I said before, I didn't know what being a Negro, or colored, or African-American was all about until much later on in my life. The only time it became an issue at that time, was when my sister went to the march on Washington, D.C. in 1963 with my aunt's church and I was upset because I was too young to take the trip, not because of the racial climate in the country.

Our schools were "segregated" by law, and the funny thing about it was that they had built two schools that looked exactly alike, in two different parts of the town, for the younger children to attend. But they had allowed some black children to attend the white school and vice versa, depending upon where you lived. By 1964, when the Civil Rights Act had been officially passed, they decided to blend everyone together and we attended school with the other little white children in town.

There were never any real issues with race and we seemed to get along together well with everyone—at least I did. My big brothers were sports stars and I became a cheerleader in High School. I still keep in touch with many of the people with whom I attended school over 60 years ago. That is how close we were as friends.

Amityville was an idyllic place with its lakes and beach, parks and stores, and children riding their bikes all over. You could leave your house in the morning, tell your parents you'd be over so-and-so's house and then return home that evening (before the streetlights came on, of course) without any serious problems. My mother did warn me about the local "weirdos" but, we just knew who and what to avoid, at all costs for our own safety. You could probably count the number of "sex offenders" who lived there on one hand.

I have many, many stories to tell about my childhood that would probably fill a book like this to the brim. But, the one that sticks out in my mind the most was what happened to me while I was attending Catechism Class for my First Communion, because we were Catholic. One of the little girls who sat next to me in  the church (shout out to LeeAnne Ireland) asked me one day, "Why is your skin so dirty?" Apparently, she had never been so close to a Black person before...we were seven years old at the time. I never forgot it because my answer to her was, "It's not dirty...I take baths." I just told her the truth.

But, the question and the incident stayed in my mind because it disturbed me so deeply that someone could have been so "ignorant" as to ask someone that kind of question. Of course, she didn't know any better at the time, but it opened my eyes to certain other things that were going on under the surface in our town. Despite the fact that Amityville had been integrated and was a mixed community for what turns out to be a 400-year history—since the 1600s when the white settlers mixed with the Native Americans and other free blacks that had lived there for centuries—there was an "undercurrent" going on, just like it was all over Long Island. But, for the most part, we lived, worked, played, loved and associated with the people around us in PEACE AND HARMONY.

That was the point that I wanted to make with this story.

My mother and father both worked for Fairchild Hiller (formerly The Republic Aircraft Co.) in Farmingdale, where they made airplanes for a living for the government. We were technically "middle-class" seemingly just like everyone else who lived around us. Amityville had its poorer sections, and it had its richer sections, but we seemed to know by instinct where to go and where to avoid to stay out of trouble. I was never called any derogatory names by any other child or adult, and I grew up thinking that I could do whatever I wanted to do in life; that the world was my oyster and that I could succeed without fear. All I had to do was excel in school (which I did), and everything else would fall magically into place.

Unfortunately, as it has been shown with what is going on today, sometimes just having a dream is not enough. When drugs and prostitution and violence took over our neighborhoods, the American Dream of owning a nice home and raising your children in a clean, safe environment seemed to fly out of the window. The crack cocaine epidemic decimated our dreams and stole the lives of many people through incarceration and addiction. But Amityville continued to be the safe haven and cultural haven it had always been, because of the many outlets like the Amityville Beach Concerts, and other local venues where people of all races, creeds and colors could let themselves go and enjoy just being alive.

In 1974, Ronald DeFeo killed his entire family and put Amityville on the map, and almost 50 years later that is all that Amityville is known for. I've traveled across the country and lived in several states, and every time I have to tell someone where I am from, they all asked me the same thing, "So is the whole town haunted, or what?" The question would make my blood boil because I knew that it wasn't true, and just the mere implication that our beautiful town was being looked at like some crazy horror movie (of which they made eleven movies and at least five books about the murders) irked me to no end. I couldn't stand it anymore.

So, I wrote my own book. It's actually not the full story about the wonderful people of Amityville like this one. It is about the infinite level of talent and famous people who have lived in and loved Amityville just like me. You would be surprised at the number of famous musicians, actors, singers, athletes, politicians and statesmen who have claimed Amityville as their home town. The "friendly village by the bay" is proud to claim these people as their own.

I have not visited home since 2009, because it was too painful to see all of the changes that have not truly benefitted the town or its ambiance. I pray that the ugliness of the world will not change the hearts of those who call Amityville home. We all know what "can't we all just get along" means in the truest sense of the words. I will always love my home town, and I truly miss going down to Tanner Park and "...sitting by the dock of the bay, just watching the tide as it rolls away." (As Otis Redding said it best in 1967.)

FAMILY STORIES

ELEANOR FALKENBACH, AN AMITYVILLE RESIDENT FROM 1929–81

by Susie Falkenbach Welch

My mother was one of The Greatest Generation—those who went through both the Great Depression and World War II. Throughout her life she was an avid writer, including an effort at writing some of her memories of her childhood. She also told a great many stories of her childhood, particularly to me. Interspersed with my recollections of her stories and research of the facts of the times are her written memories—memories of a full life with hardships and rewards, sorrows and successes. She seemed to take it all in stride and was grateful for the many blessings of her life. She considered one of those blessings to be the 51 years that she was an Amityville resident.

On August 17, 1921, World War I was over, the Veteran's Bureau had been created, and women had been granted the right to vote the year before. America was in its second year of 13 years of Prohibition. Harding was President and Coolidge was Vice President. A loaf of bread cost 10 cents, a gallon of gas was 11 cents, the price of a new Ford was $420, an ounce of gold cost $20.67, the average price of a new home was just over $7,000, and the Dow Jones Index was 73 points…and on that day, my mother, Eleanor McAlester, was born in Mineola, New York.

In 1929, when my mother was only seven years old, her mother died, and she went to live with Axel and Carolina, her maternal grandparents. By then, Axel and

Carolina had built a house in Amityville that was adjacent to the land that would become Zahn's Airport just a few years later. In the new house, they had room for both their grown and, as yet, unmarried daughter, Louise, and now their little granddaughter Eleanor, too. Axel was a cabinetmaker and carpenter by trade, but by the time he and his wife lived in Amityville, he was in his mid-60s, retired, and worked around his small chicken and produce farm. Also, he was often known to be out in his shed or barn, working on some kind of gadget or invention or pursuing his hobby of crafting ship models.

Axel drove a little Ford truck to deliver his eggs and broilers, and to pick up the baby chicks when they arrived from Maryland at the post office. The boxes of chicks were full of breathing holes and the peeping was considerable. Then my mother, little Eleanor, would go out to the chicken house where the brooders had been set up to keep the chicks warm. She remembered that "it sure did get stuffy in those hen houses." She and her grandfather would take each little yellow chick and dip its bill into water to teach it to drink. It was only a few weeks later when her grandmother heated the water for the big washtubs. Her grandfather would take each of the broilers, one by one, and slit their throats, and then hang them by the feet in the surrounding trees while they fluttered their lives away. Her grandmother would put them in the hot water and begin to pluck the feathers. Smelling wet chicken feathers when she was growing up was not my mother's favorite memory! After the chickens were cleaned, her grandmother would cut off their feet and clean them and then boil them in a pot to obtain a gelatinous liquid. Did she use it as stock for the basis of soup? My mother did not remember. What she did remember was that it was "Chicken Every Sunday," just like the book with that title.

When my mother moved to Amityville with her grandparents, she continued her schooling at the Park Avenue school building, which had been built in 1894. In later years, it was known as Park North because two more school buildings, Park

South and Park Central, were built on that land. My mother was placed in third grade.

In her memoirs, she wrote about her school years. One of her favorite teachers was Miss Lappine. Miss Lappine later became Mrs. Ira Chichester, received her degree in Library Science, and continued her employment and residence in Amityville. My mother also fondly remembered a popular janitor called Pop Smith. He kept the wide wooden floors smelling clean and sanitary by pushing a dry green sawdust-like cleaner with his wide push broom around the halls and classrooms. Years later she could still picture Pop with the large bottles of ink he brought to the teachers to be dispensed into the glass inkwells in each student's desk. The gym classes were held in the second floor gymnasium. At recess time, and sometimes after lunch, the kids played Hide 'n Seek or King of the Hill, standing on the cement crypts of the cemetery behind the Park North building. Those remains were moved a number of years later to a cemetery elsewhere in the Town of Babylon. The kids who brought their lunch sat on rows of plain backless benches in the basement lunchroom. There was a small cafeteria where lunch could be purchased, and she remembered the lingering food odors as the ceilings were very low so the cooking odors did not readily escape. The basement was also used for drying the clothing of those who arrived soaked on a rainy or snowy day. The teachers and school nurse always saw to it that wet shoes and clothing were sent below. In the winter, the smell of wet wool permeated that close warm area.

My mother did well in school, particularly in her English courses and, in high school, her business courses, too. In those years, business courses were usually called commercial courses. In her teen years, she wrote a great many poems, and at least five of them were published in a regional newspaper of years ago, the *Long Island Sun*. When she was fifteen and a freshman in high school, she met the love of her life, an "older" man—a senior in Amityville High School, Hans Falkenbach.

She wrote that when the new high school was built next door, she was a freshman and a tall senior boy, who was on the wrestling team, always singled her out to talk with her in the hall of the two-story, 1932 building. Classes were on the first or second floor, and the gymnasium on the second floor was shared by all, for the wrestling matches and both girls' and boys' basketball teams. It also became the ballroom for the senior prom. The senior boy asked her, the freshman, if she would go to the dance with him as many of his senior friends were going, too. She was fifteen, and it was her first date. The music was supplied by a DJ, and the gym was decorated with balloons and a serve-yourself punch bowl with some assorted cookies.

My mother, now nicknamed Ellie, and my dad, Hans, continued to date for the next three years. Eventually, she decided to graduate a semester early so she could go to work, make some money, and get married. She had held a secretarial job in a Suffolk County office in the summer of 1938, and with that job reference, her secretarial skills, and a high school diploma, she found a job in the Garment District of New York City. Thus in January 1939, she started commuting into New York on the Long Island Railroad. She was dressed in the clothing for a working girl then, which included gloves, a hat, high heels, and of course stockings with a seam up the back of the leg! She was paid $16 per week, gave $4 a week to her grandmother for room and board, paid $4 a week to the LIRR, and kept the fabulous sum of $8 a week for herself. Incidentally, that $16 a week was both her gross pay and net pay because my mother's boss paid her under the table! She explained that besides Federal Income Tax, Social Security deductions had begun; and many employers were trying to avoid paying those taxes on their employees. She was 17 ½ years old. I believe accepting that method of salary is the only crime my mother ever committed! She said that although the Great Depression was said to be over, she still saw the "bread lines" in the city in 1939.

Ellie Falkenbach on the far left with her Junior League friends in 1946.

After saving some money, my parents got married the next year, in June 1940, in the Simpson Methodist Church in Amityville. They had a three-day honeymoon in a lean-to on Hunter Mountain in the Catskills, and then they settled down to live in the apartment that Hans had fashioned out of a bedroom in his mother's house on Morris Street. Next they rented a house on a canal on Bayside Place for a few years and started their family. During those years with a young family, my mother was also involved in Amityville life, including the Junior League, an organization of women dedicated to promoting and improving the community.

In 1949, they bought a house that would become their family home for over 30 years—123 South Bayview Avenue. What a convenient spot that was! Walking or driving two blocks south brought the family to the Amityville Public Beach on the Great South Bay and the village boat launch as well. A few blocks north would soon be the site of the new high school, where Ellie would later be working in the school district offices and the girls would attend high school. The property they purchased had a Tudor style house on it, built in the 1920s, plus a large detached garage, and a plot of land across the back of the property that became a prolific garden and source of quite a variety of produce. The days of canning would never be over for some people who wanted to preserve fruits and vegetables. Freezing produce, however, was now an easier option to canning, that intense laboring to prepare foods to be put into specially sterilized and sealed glass jars to store for the winter months. Most of the produce from my dad's garden was quickly blanched, sealed in bags, stored in special boxes and marked, and put in a deep freezer.

After my sister, Carol, and I were in school all day, our mother went back to work in a local company. Then in 1952, she accepted a secretarial position in the Amityville public schools. In a few years, she was promoted to be the Business Office Supervisor. A few years after that, she was appointed as the Clerk of the Board of Education—a second and separate job which included preparing agendas, taking and transcribing minutes, and supervising school board elections. She took accounting courses at Farmingdale Aggie (now State College at Farmingdale) to give herself more skills and confidence in her business office responsibilities. In one course, the professor asked her to teach a particular class because he realized that she knew more about the topic than he did. She became an active member in the NYS chapter of the Association of School Business Officials (ASBO) and traveled to state conferences and workshops in Albany and elsewhere in the state. She also traveled out of state to national conferences. She became well-known in the NYS Education Department in Albany as a person to call to ask how she handled various accounting issues unique to school district finances. She held both of her positions until she retired in 1980. By that time, the Park North building had been renovated as Administration Offices for the Amityville school district, and my mother's office was located on the spot where her third grade classroom had been in 1929. At her retirement dinner, she said, "…and now I have come full circle."

In 1981, Hans and Ellie moved to Sarasota, Florida. They had already started spending their summers in the little chalet that Hans had built for them in the picturesque Rangeley Lakes Region in the mountains of Western Maine. They continued with that lifestyle until Hans passed away in Rangeley in 2002. They had dated for three years, been married for 62 years, and so had been together for 65 years. Soon Ellie moved from Sarasota to St. Augustine, Florida, near her youngest daughter, me, but was able to spend summers in Maine through her 90th birthday in 2011.

Through those years that they no longer lived in Amityville, Hans and Ellie continued to visit Amityville to see their friends and also hosted them in Rangeley and Sarasota. They also attended a number of Amityville reunions in a variety of places on the East Coast. It seems evident that for many former Amityville residents, an old expression could be applied…you can take the people out of Amityville, but you can't take Amityville out of the people.

THE INFLUENCE OF THE GREAT SOUTH BAY

THE INFLUENCE OF
THE GREAT SOUTH BAY

What's Going On Over There?

by Rudy Sittler, Jr.

July 1947, 176 Ocean Avenue, Amityville, N.Y. The home of Mary and F.C. Morrell, my grandparents home since 1929. This was the view from my bedroom window, Island #2 in the Amityville River, painted by my grandmother. We had just moved back from Chicago and were temporarily staying here until we found a house. We being my father Rudy Sittler, Sr., my mother Rebecca, my brother Peter and my sister, Sandy, who was four months old.

I had a whole month to kill until school started and I was more than a little curious as to what was happening on that island. I got up my courage, jumped in my grandfather's rowboat and paddled over. When I landed, there was a door open in front of me so I went in. I found myself in a machine shop with a lathe, drill press, blow torches and all kinds of tools. Metal filings of brass were all over the floor. I heard hammering in the next room so I proceeded through another doorway and was in a large room with two men pounding boat nails into the bottom of an upside-down sailboat. They were planking a "Tuck." They both gave me a look, then went right on hammering. Finally they got to a stopping point and Wilbur says to Jimmy, "Well what do we have here?" This was the beginning of a lifelong association with the Narrasketuck Class sailboat that continues to this day. Jimmy Ketcham, who had raised three sons, came right over and started asking me questions. I was ten years old and scared to death, but I didn't know what a 'tuck was or who Wilbur Ketcham was.

Painting by M. Morrell, Feb. 1949, depicting Wilbur Ketcham and "Pal" with his Amityville River boatyard workshop and home of the Narrasketuck Class sailboat on Island #2 in the background.

In 1947 it was a full-service boatyard and they had boats outside waiting in the water, and on the railways, to be serviced. They were building three 'tucks between paying jobs. Usually boat building was done in the winter, but in 1947 the Narrasketuck Class was hot. Race week had 47 'tucks in two divisions on Monday, August 4th on the starting line off Timber Point. Wilbur had put the Narrasketuck plans (his design) on sale for $10 per set so anyone could build their own 'tuck. Asa Smith built 11 'tucks in 1947 alone.

OLD GUYS TEACH A KID

by Kurt Nezbeda

1950. A cardboard box 8′ x 3′ x 2′ appears at our garage door. The five-year-old Kid rubs his stubby, grubby fingers across the lettering: "U-Make-It-Kit-Boat". "It's an eight-foot dinghy, son. Let's build it together." With a blunt, front transom, there's no wasted space that it would normally have if it were pointy. The Kid "helped." Counted out the screws and nails in the kit and laid them out in neat rows. Completed, the "pram" would feature in many of the Kid's adventures for the next 20 years.

1953. The Kid is eight years old. Dad has bought a 1938 Chris Craft cabin cruiser. He keeps it at Bill Terry's boat yard on Ketchum Avenue. He goes to work on it in the spring. The Kid and a huge lunch go with him. The Kid is supposed to "help." Bored, the Kid "helps" as requested by finding loose nails in the boat yard's dirt. Bangs them straight with an old hammer and lays them in neat rows. In case "someone needs them."

Ketchum Creek was not built over in those days. An eight-year-old Kid and a pram could explore, play pirate, chase ducks, and generally amuse himself on the water. No worries about the Kid drowning. Young "Water Ratz" are taught to swim at an early age. The water is also shallow. "Stay within earshot in case Mr. Terry's father-in-law needs you."

"Tweet!! Hey Kid, bear a hand!" An old guy needs help moving a boat. Old school. Bottle jacks, levers, fulcrums, and rollers did the work then, moving six-ton cruisers; work that Travel Lifts do now. Really simple. Old guy places a block and bottle jack beneath a keel or winter cradle. A couple of pumps and the assembly is lifted enough for a small boy to squirt under and place a log roller. More rollers follow. Two long levers and the old guy and the boy can move almost anything over relatively level ground. Slowly. Carefully. Onto a flat bed cart with railroad wheels. The rails go into the water. A marine railway.

Pulleys and cables lead into a shed. An ancient gasoline engine stands ready. Cast iron, one cylinder, piston the size of a paint can, spoked flywheel the size of a wagon wheel. The old guy primes it with gas, rocks the flywheel to and fro a few times and, standing onto one of the spokes, spins it. The engine catches. "Puff... chuga...chuga...chuga...puff!" All of three horsepower. REAL horses. Clydesdales. In the Fall it will pull the heaviest boats from the water. Slowly. Carefully. Sixty odd years on, this Kid, now an old guy, would love to have it for his motor collection.

Tired of straightening nails, the Kid finds four old guys gathered under a tree. Supervising. A paper bag with a bottle passes among them. "Hey Kid! Wadda ya doin', commeeea."

"Gee, what's in the bottle?"

"Refreshments."

"Gee, can I have some?"

"Ahhh, I dunno you'd like this. Kinda tastes like medicine. Tell ya what, see those ducks over there? You row over there in your pram and whack one on the head and bring it to us we'll buy you a Coke. We're old guys and we can't catch 'em anymore, and we haven't had any duck meat in a long time."

The other old guys nod assent. The Kid clambers into the dink. The old guys watch, elbows nudge, the bag makes another circuit.

The Kid rows towards the ducks. The ducks have seen the Kid before. Old guys watch from shore, sure that the Kid will flail; fail and fall into the water. Some folks amuse easily.

Now at the flock, within oar range, the Kid stands and, like Casey at The Bat, delivers a mighty swat! SPLASH! Water flying! QUAWAAWAAWAACK! The ducks explode into the air, roar past the old guys who all raise their arms as if holding imaginary pump shotguns, swinging as if drawing a bead…"BANG… chuck, chuck…BANG…chuck, chuck…BANG BANG BANG!" they all mouth.

No ducks fall to their imaginary shots. "Stu, ya never could hit squat anyways."

No ducks were injured by the oar. The miss was intentional. The ducks were the Kid's buddies. The Kid did not fall overboard. Much to the chagrin of the old guys. A few more nudges, the bag passes around once more.

Chandleries sell all manner of nautical items. Geegaws, fancy clothing, designer jewelry, brass shiny objects and maybe things you might use on your yacht. The boat yard had a ship's store. It sold only boat stuff: cleats, screws, paint, shackles and hardware. The Kid had a grand time playing with the inventory. He was easily amused. Still is.

The ship's store sold rope. Three strand Manila. Tough, stiff stuff. Not like the limp-wristed nylon they use today. Spools hung in the attic and the ends of the ropes dropped through holes in the ceiling. Whoever was running the store would pull, measure and cut as many feet as the customer wanted.

Rope is the stuff that comes off the spool. When put to use it becomes line. Bow line, dock line, etc. The rope makers claim that tying knots in it might somehow weaken it. The elegant way of working it is to use a pointed stick, called a fid, to unwrap or unlay the strands and weave other strands into it. In this way rope ends could be treated to prevent unlaying, make "eyes," or join two lengths together. It's called splicing. While "splicing the main brace," a nautical term meaning they passed that bag around, the same old guys taught the Kid how to splice…rope.

In the spring, not so old guys would come into the ship's store to buy stuff. Some of them "tawked" funny, kinda honked. They had newer boats. Generally hadn't learned how to handle them. Lots of Zoom Zoom Slam Slam when docking. Cigars, loud clothing, gold necklaces and pinky rings. The old guys said they were city guys. The Kid got to know them a bit and could imitate the accent, to the amusement of the old guys with the paper bag, and the city guys too. Kids can get away with a lot.

"Ehh, I see some of these ropes got fancy loops on the ends. Where do youse get 'em?"

"See the little blond Kid in the dinghy, he charges a quarter a splice."

On a good afternoon the Kid could make two bucks, and have all the soda he wanted. Dad and the old guys chuckled in amusement. Mom was maybe not so pleased. "Kid's gotta learn, Honey."

Thanks, guys.

BOATING

by Ted Crocker

Growing up in Amityville meant being close to the water and boating. My first boat as a teen was a 1950s, sixteen-foot Thompson lapstrake build. My dad bought it for my brother and me to fix up, which gave us a sense of respect plus some great bonding. Add a 35-horse Johnson and we were free to explore the Great South Bay! It seemed that Dad always had a boat, so we knew the water and boat safety and etiquette.

Over the years I pretty much lived with a canal out my back door and a number of boats docked there. At one point I had a 1968 28′ Trojan cabin cruiser with a flying bridge (teak and mahogany), a 16′ tunnel hull hydroplane that did 50 mph and a brand new 18′ Chris Craft ski boat bought at the boat show, all docked out back. This when I lived right up the street, and canal, from Dick & Dora's restaurant.

We would often do a slow cruise up and down the canals looking at homes and boats we would never be able to afford. Beer and wine might have been included…

Some of my fondest memories were having a bunch of friends on the Trojan and going crabbing under the Robert Moses bridge. I rigged up a bunch of car headlights mounted inside cut-off bleach bottles and hooked up to car batteries with big alligator clips. The crabs were attracted to the lights and swam toward them.

No lie, when I say that besides using nets, we could get on the swim platform and grab crabs by hand. Once ashore we had a crab party, cooking and cleaning them. Once done, and after eating as much as we could, there was still a mountain of crabmeat on the table. Everyone got to take home fresh crab meat!

I miss crab spaghetti sauce and crab daiquiris. Living on a canal you could go out at night with a flashlight and find crabs on the side of your dock for a great dinner!

Also, we could take our boats near the flats, jump in and dig up clams with our feet. I also miss clam spaghetti sauce and clam daiquiris.

On my little Chris Craft I had a short (36-inch) Shakespeare reel and fishing pole and I always had canned clams onboard to use as bait when I saw a group of boats fishing on my way to Gilgo. I wonder if the waters behind Amityville still have that bounty of crabs, clams and fish?

I also did a lot of sailboating out of Narrasketuck Yacht Club at the end of Berger Ave, across from Bud Aboumrad and remember stepping the mast of an 18′ Hobie Cat each time we launched it at the beach, near where the firemen practiced for tournaments and we played softball.

WINTER ON THE AMITYVILLE RIVER

by Doug Robinson, an excerpt from his book
My Amityville, Memories of a Golden Time

It seemed like winters were colder when we were young. About one out of every two or three years the river froze over and we went ice skating in back of our Ocean Avenue house. The official, unofficial, ice tester was Mr. Ronback from across the river. He would walk out on the new ice with a three foot long log and thump the end of the log on the ice to make sure it was safe. Only when he gave the signal were we allowed to skate.

Mom and Dad would put out the word the ice was safe and our house became ice skating central. All my friends would get delivered to our house and use our kitchen or back steps to lace up. We kept a long wooden plank that stretched from the dock to the ice as a ramp to get on the ice.

We spent most of the time organizing teams and playing hockey. A four foot board was our goal and the shouts of "no lifting" filled the crisp air. The puck had to hit the board to count as a goal. One of the hazards we faced was losing pucks. Because the ice would rise and fall with the tide, the ice along the docks would break up so errant passes might find their way to the edge of the ice and the bottom of the river. We always kept a crab net handy to rescue those pucks, with varying degrees of success. Many a hockey game was cut short after the only puck was lost.

The scourge of our makeshift hockey rinks was the eelers. They would work their way down the river with bushel baskets, axes and long eel spears, cutting holes in the ice and working through the holes with the spears. They would do this every 20 feet or so leaving behind a path of open holes and chunks of ice. It is amazing how many pucks you could lose though an 18 inch diameter hole. And the next day the ice chunks would be frozen to the surface and pose a tripping hazard. The trick was to follow the eelers and kick the ice chunks back in the hole so they would refreeze overnight.

Many a day the river came to life with hundreds of skaters and looked like a Currier & Ives etching. I always loved to watch the iceboats, mostly home made using two wooden planks fashioned in the form of a cross, fitted with runners and sails borrowed from sail boats. These were extremely fast and equally dangerous.

One of the gym teachers had a small hand held sail. He would use the sail much like a modern day wind surfer but with no board, just a pair of ice skates. He could do just about everything an ice boater could do but without the boat.

Mom and Dad would stand watch from the kitchen or sun porch. The kitchen became the snack bar as we would warm up at lunch time with a hot bowl of soup or finish the day with a steaming cup of hot chocolate. The kitchen was also the first aid station for the inevitable bangs and scrapes and the communications center for phoning for rides home. It was always busy because all the parents knew their kids would be safe at our house and Mom and Dad made it a fun place to be.

For my 60th birthday my sons put together a book for me with pictures of my sixty years and collected stories about me from the family. Cousin Sara (Adams) Acton contributed the following:

"Some of my fondest memories are of ice skating behind the house on Ocean Avenue. We could never wait until the canal froze. Then all of Doug's friends and all of my friends would skate behind the house and Gracie [Doug's mom] would have many of us to the house for hot chocolate. I loved to warm up over the huge heating vent near the stairs."

SAILING AND GUNNING, TWO YEARS

by Rudy Sittler, Jr., excerpts from his unpublished memoir,
Narrasketuck Scrapbook

Early June 1953

My father, Rudy Sittler, Sr., Gil Haight, George Colyer, Jr. and Sr., and myself, Rudy, Jr., went down to the Three Mile Harbor, in the Peconic Bays, to Bob Story's Boatyard, with Arthur Robbins, who drove us, to pick up Gil Haight's new yacht and bring it back to Amityville. This yacht was called the *ATOM* and was formerly the *Commodore*, built in Amityville in 1913 by the Wicks Brothers. This yacht had full-length planking with no butt blocks in its 54-foot length. I never saw Gil do anything but vacuum out the bilge. The ribs were three inches square with copper rivets. The sides of the cabin were African mahogany two inches thick. The keel was a single piece of Long Island oak. The first thing Gil did was pry off the sign board and restore her rightful name. We left the Three Mille Harbor at 5:00 a.m., sailed East, and rounded Montauk Point by 8:00 a.m., through the Shinnecock Canal by noon, down the bay and home by 7:00 p.m.

Pirate #19

While we were at Story's Boatyard we spotted a Narrasketuck sailboat under a canvas. Turns out it's *Aloha*, #19. It was built by Bill Carl in 1937–38. Herb Latchaw owned it but had recently died and his widow wanted to sell it for $300.

Less than a week later it was over on Island #2 in Amityville. Now, I have to say a word about my father. He was not the 1950s typical father. He was the guy that taught me how to drive a car while sitting on his lap and couldn't reach the pedals with my feet. He was the guy that bought me a Seaford Skiff from Paul Ketcham in 1948 when I was 11 years old

and shoved me off the Ocean Avenue dock and said "sail." He was the guy who threw me into a pool and said "swim" before I was walking. Anyway, he and Gil said nothing to me about buying #19 and somehow getting it over to Wilbur's Island. This was an era when trailers were a rare sight. Wooden boats had to be kept in the water. Jimmy and Wilbur (Ketcham) gave #19 the once-over and told me what to do to get her ready for racing. She had one good set of Ratseys (sails) with blue numbers, and one old flat set. I started working hard to get ready for Race Week. I'm not sure how #19 got the name *Pirate*. Wilbur used to call me that, but it could have been Marion Haight. The picture is George Colyer and me rigging #19 for the first time.

Commodore, Blown High And Dry, Awaits Dredger

Gilgo Island Storm

One last little note on this year of 1953. On November 6th, the Colyers, Jr. and Sr., myself and Gil Haight were on the *Commodore* over in the old Gilgo channel for the opening of gunning season. We were anchored under the lee of Gilgo Island in a light North wind. During the night the wind suddenly hauled around to the Southeast and started to blow. We put out another anchor and bridled it with the Danforth we had out, but to no avail. The wind was so strong that it pulled one of the cleats out of the deck and we were soon on one hook. It didn't take long for

Watercolor by Rudy Sittler, Sr. Amityville's main canal. Family boat *Betty Anne* in foreground with Wilbur Ketcham's new house on the left and my grandparents' house in the middle. Frank and Mary Morrell, 176 Ocean Ave. Schwindler's boathouse on the right, and the *U-52* in front (our old boat said to be sold to someone in Bellport).

the remaining hawser to saw through despite attempts to wrap it. Twang, off on a Nantucket Sleigh Ride to fetch up on Gilgo Island. But the old *Commodore* was up to the task. She ground to a halt as light as a feather, so we all went back to sleep. The next day was a sight I have never seen before or since. All the islands in the bay were covered with water. It looked like a giant lake. There was only a thin dune line along the beach separating the ocean and the bay and it was like a piece of glass. It took the Ronbacks two weeks to dredge her off.

Amityville, L.I.,1954

This is about growing up as a boy on the Great South Bay. The summer time was sailing every weekend at a different town along the bay. It was a real family thing to do. Everybody was involved and it was like a summer long vacation. You would have the boat packed and ready to go on Friday night. You would pile on board, pick up Dad from the Long Island Rail Road, get the Narrasketuck sailboats all hooked up for towing, and go off to whatever weekend regatta was on the schedule. (Babylon, Bay Shore, Timber Pt., Wet Pants, Point O Woods, Domino, Bellport, Westhampton). I would sail the 'tuck with my girlfriend and my father; my brother Peter, with his outboard, would run errands for people in the fleet, getting blocks of ice and papers, helped by little sister Sandy, and my poor mother got to stay on board and dry all the wet clothes and keep us together. Oh, and she wrote down the scores for our fleet as they finished. Because the 'tuck and star fleets were so big, several people kept scores which they analyzed after the race.

Jimmy's Shack

In the winter time I was interested in going duck hunting or "gunning" as it was called. My father wasn't really into freezing his butt off in a leaky duck boat so he took me over to Gilgo Island one day in November of 1948.

I saw this old RR lineman's shack at the South Side of Gilgo Island and soon I was standing on shore with my 16-gauge single-barreled Savage shotgun on my shoulder waving goodbye to Dad. This shack was owned and occupied by one James H. Ketcham.

Ketcham was a retired USCG Chief Bosuns Mate and lifelong bayman. Of course I knew him from Wilbur's Island. Jim and Wilbur built the 'tucks. He told me to get into the shack by the stove and warm up. Seeing as I was dressed in a surplus navy pea coat and Levi jeans, it didn't take me long to accept. He took my gun and greased it up with Hoppes gun grease and hung it over the door next to two Parker guns, a 10-gauge and a 12-gauge. Then Jim said, "Well, let's see if I can't fix you up here." He told me to get a pair of long johns before I came out again and then gave me a pair of hip boots, a pair of waterproof pants cut off at the knees, and a waterproof windbreaker. Then I got a duck hunting cap to hide that shock of bright blonde hair I had at that time. Jimmy's gunning boat was a double-man skiff with sloped sides, and two ash shoving poles that were our sole means of propulsion. Decoys were made of cork with heads made by Jimmy himself. He could carve a broadbill's head in about 20 minutes out of sugar pine. This boat was also fitted with a sprit and sail, but were seldom used. We needed the room for PAL, Jimmy's dog.

PALS

Jim had this dog named PAL. He was a big red setter. Of course Wilbur had a big red setter named PAL, too, and so did Honey Axtmann. When these guys got together the stories would be told about how smart their dog PAL was. Why, Jim's PAL was so smart that Jimmy told me he went gunning once and had his 10-gauge gun but brought the 12-gauge ammunition. So he told PAL to go back to the Coast Guard station and get his other gun from behind the door and don't you know, an hour later he came back with the right gun. Of course, I believed this and everything else Jimmy ever told me. This I didn't see. PAL came with us in the gunning skiff. If we shot a bird down he was out there in a flash to pick it up. If we shot more than one down he would get confused and go to the closest bird, but if he saw another one he let the first one go, then try to get the second one. Eventually getting all in. Also at night he slept at the bottom of the bunk and kept your feet warm.

Clamming

Jim's PAL could dig clams. In front of the shack was a clam bed that Jimmy kept seeding in the summer so when gunning season came around there were always clams available. Now, if we wanted clams for dinner, Jim would put his boots on and wade into the clam bed. He'd yell at PAL "go under my boot, PAL, under my boot." PAL would jump in and start digging a hole with his hind legs. Of

course everything on the bottom came up on the bank but plenty of clams came with it.

This I saw.

Parkers

Of vital importance to these old baymen were their guns. They all had Parkers. Most of them bought them from the Parker Co. back in the 20s and 30s. They came in different grades and were priced according to the engraving and walnut stocks. All the one's I saw were double-barreled shotguns. When I got older, my father gave me a double gun. Parkers were no longer made, so I wound up with an L.C. Smith. A lot of these Parkers had Damascus steel barrels. When the new powder came out in the high brass shells, some of these gun barrels couldn't take it. So a lot of the old-timers stuck to low brass shells and smokeless powder. However, one old timer named Honey Axtmann decided he was going to stick to the old black powder and load his own shells. So Jimmy and I would be up on Gilgo somewhere and the sun would be coming up and BOOM, this cloud of black smoke would show itself to the East of us and Jimmy would say, "Well, I guess Honey and Wibur must be over to goose flats."

Stories

Back in the old days when guns were muzzle loaded and Jim was goose shooting out on Porpoise Bar, Jim was pounding some shot down the barrel when he heard a flock come over. He got excited and left the ramrod in the barrel. He shot one with that ramrod going thru him just like an arrow.

Or the time they were rigged out in the wide place on Gilgo and a dense fog came in. Jim had tied the duck boat to a shoving pole stuck vertically in a marsh.

They could hear the geese all around them, but couldn't see to shoot.

Suddenly a flock came over and WHAP, a big goose dropped dead at Jims feet.

He had flown right into that vertical shoving pole and broke his neck.

Cooking

Jim told me you only needed three things to become a good cook; onions, salt pork, and potatoes. I also remember a bag of flour because Jim used to make dumplings and he would flower the clams, oysters, and eels before frying them up. These things didn't need refrigeration and he had a box in the window that he stored them in. Also it was winter. There was a pot on the stove that was always cooking. You would just add whatever you needed. Mrs. Ketcham would send out beach plum

jam and big ginger cookies. Other dishes were "Fire Island Hoorah," "Offshore Stew," and "Shelldrake Pot Pie." He had a big silver milk can outside that was filled with water. There were bunk beds on the west wall, one upper and a double down below. Jimmy never locked this shack when he was ashore. He just put a peg on the door handle in case anyone got stuck out there with a bottle of Rock Rye on the table.

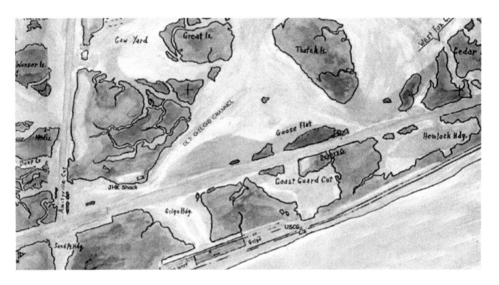

Old Bay Places

The islands in Great South Bay are loaded with colorful names and places such as "the Grouts," "the Cow Pasture," "the Haul," "Goose Flats," etc. How they got these names and who named them is lost to the ages as one generation passes this information down to the next. This part of the world has probably changed the least in the past 100 years, but with the influx of more and more people, boats, and, worse, wave runners, I hope the bay can hang in there.

THE INFLUENCE OF THE GREAT SOUTH BAY

SUMMERTIME IN AMITYVILLE IN THE 1950S

by Lynn Darling Hendershot

Growing up in Amityville, NY, on the Great South Bay, we could hardly wait for Memorial Day, the official start of summer fun! Swimming and boating were, of course, the favorite pastimes.

I learned to swim at the Amityville Village Beach. Although my father was an excellent swimmer and had spent his childhood swimming the Amityville canals, he hired Jim Hicks to teach me. I'm not sure what his "day job" was, but he taught me well. The big prize was being allowed to swim out to the float. Although I was met by an army of "green flies," the feeling of accomplishment was worth it!

My dad bought a boat, which could only be described as a large rowboat with a very heavy, slow, engine on the back. My mother did not enjoy the ride, so my dad and I would head out of the Amityville River into the Great South Bay looking for good clamming spots. We would jump into the water and work our toes into the slimy muck feeling for something hard. Once found, we would dive under and scoop up the muddy, hard-shell creatures…hoping for the delectable Little Necks or Cherrystones. The big chowder clams were brought home as well, as we knew my mother would make Manhattan Clam Chowder for dinner.

When my parents moved to the south part of Amityville, within walking distance of Unqua Corinthian Yacht Club, I begged them to join, which they did, but without the "Yacht" part. From age 12, my days were spent practicing with the Unqua swim team in the morning, lunch at the snack bar and sailing lessons on the

Blue Jay, the Club's boat, in the afternoon. Although not a 'star' swimmer, it was fun swimming against other Long Island Clubs and perfecting my stroke. I can still hear Coach Nick yelling "pull!" at me!

There were always boys and girls hanging out in the Junior Corinthian Clubhouse where I learned to perfect the art of ping pong, (playing against the boys) as well as Crazy Eights and Knuckles! If we were lucky, some days the boys with power boats would show up at the dock looking for "crew" to go across the Bay to the "heading" at West Gilgo Beach for a swim in the ocean. If we were really lucky, one of these boys would offer to use up all his gas trying to teach us how to waterski!

As a senior in high school, armed with my Senior Lifesaving credential, thanks to Jean Gregory's expert training, I returned to the Amityville Village Beach, this time as a swimming instructor. I am so grateful for the life skills learned and the friendships made during those summers in Amityville! They were special times with special people!

CRABBING

by Judy Renz Smutny

Growing up on Long Island, specifically Amityville, we took many things for granted. It wasn't until my later years that I realized how lucky we were. We took for granted that we experienced all four season; living in Miami for the past 42 years has made me appreciate the time spent in Amityville, especially the fall. We had it all, hurricanes, blizzards, blistering summer heat, and soggy spring thaws.

My fondest memories are from the warm summer nights that we would spend crabbing on the dock where Ocean Avenue and Richmond Avenue met. We would load up the car with all the necessary gear and a few snacks. My father would take a fishing pole, and my brother and I would gather the crab nets, peach baskets and string. My mother, just happy to be out in the warm summer air, simply gathered up her chair. Getting there early was important, as the best spots filled up quickly. Sometimes it was so crowded that the bulkhead space would be totally occupied. We would search the bulkhead for crabs, below the water line, and then delicately submerge our nets from far behind and attempt to scoop them up. It took some practice but eventually we would prevail. I can remember when something was caught, whether it be a fish or crab, we would scramble from place to place to get a good view of the fresh catch. Eventually my parents would say it was time to pack up and go. All the way home my brother and I would be playing with the still live crabs and giggle when one would attempt to escape. Yes, there were a few pinched fingers, but that was part of the game.

Fast forward twentyish years and a whole new way of crabbing evolved. We were young adults and in charge of our own lives. Some of us were married, some not, but we all still loved crabbing.

Now the crabbing was done on a boat, at night, and our "snacks and libation" had changed. The gear was still the same, but we needed a light to attract the crabs as they swam across the top of the water. Usually we did this on the weekend, and some of us needed a babysitter, but none of that was a problem. We would do anything necessary to get out on the bay for an evening of cool breeze and lifelong friendships. As the night wore on, the crabbing became more interesting and might even include a few people falling overboard while attempting to secure the "big one."

Once we had a sufficient amount, which was almost always, we headed home with our catch. Now the crabs had to be cleaned, and that was an art in itself. There were times we ended up running around the kitchen trying to wrangle one who had escaped. The crabs were steamed in fresh tomatoes from the garden, olive oil, garlic and parsley and then served over angel hair pasta!! We usually drank Mateus Rose with this magnificent meal. Oh the memories.

Those days will never return, but the flavors and friendships will last a lifetime. Whether we were young or old, crabbing will hold a place in our memories forever.

TWO BOYS AND A MINIMAX

by Bruce Edwards, as originally printed in *The Antique Outboarder*

Kurt Nezbeda and I grew up (a debatable term) in Amityville, Long Island, NY. Kurt's home was right on the Amityville River, which opened up to the Great South Bay, and I lived a half-block inland. At fifteen, wanting a fast boat for not much money, I built my Minimax in the winter of 1961–62. Kurt and I were always doing crazy things on the water and this fit. The plans estimated a total cost of around $20. I decided to upgrade the bottom sheet of quarter inch plywood to marine grade, which I believe was selling for around $14 per sheet. I already had some black and white paint and some fiberglass, which helped balance the cost, and I wound up spending around $25–$30. This represented a fortune to a fifteen year old!

Kurt and I launched the boat in Kurt's backyard in the spring of 1962. I had wrongly assumed that I could just use my parents' 1958 Evinrude 18 hp. My dad flatly refused, citing my safety as the reason. The Evinrude remained on his 1954 Lyman runabout. I asked Kurt if I could borrow his 1954 Evinrude 3 hp, which he had had since it was new, and he agreed to let me put it on the boat for the maiden voyage. I was thrilled with the boat's performance with only a 3 hp engine. It got right up on plane and planed well. Steering, on the other hand, was a challenge. The plans called for a flat keelson, which allowed the boat to slide unmercifully during turns. The Minimax yawed like an aircraft under full left or right rudder. The fix would have been to add a racing fin, but since I had spent every cent I had on building the boat, this was out of the question.

Kurt Nezbeda in the Minimax.

Kurt and I soon yearned for more speed. He also had a 1956 Johnson 15 hp, which we tried next. I remember being skeptical due to the fact that this was the maximum horsepower recommended for the Minimax, and I was concerned about its handling, but we tried it anyway. The Johnson worked really well. I have no idea how fast the boat would go, but it was certainly the fastest boat I had ever driven up to that point. It was strictly a straight line boat with the 3 hp and was even worse with the 15.

We enjoyed the performance of the Johnson for several weeks, but again wanted more speed. In our quest for speed, we removed the exhaust from the Johnson and replaced it with an aluminum plate and two straight aluminum exhaust tubes. The Johnson looked and sounded great but I don't think we actually picked up any significant horsepower.

Once again we felt a need for more speed. The only engine that was "available" was Kurt's father's 1959 Evinrude Lark 35 hp, however, it could only be used if his father was at work and his mother was out of the house since they surely would have objected to our using it on the Minimax. The Lark was only on the Minimax for one day, and to this day, I do not know why the transom didn't fall off. I never ran the boat with the Lark, but Kurt reported that it went "real fast." To start the motor, Kurt says, he had to get a heavy friend to sit on the very bow while he pulled on the starter cord. Steering was just barely possible if he shifted his weight, and, because there was no tiller, Kurt had to work the throttle nub with his fingers. The weight of the engine required the driver to keep as far forward until the boat planed, as it surely would have swamped.

The Minimax began having hull problems during the use of the Johnson, which increased during the use of the Lark. I vividly remember being hit with flying deck screws when I encountered chop on the Great South Bay! The fiberglass began to show serious cracks and breaks, and many of the remaining deck screws started to push their way through the fiberglass. The boat began to leak mildly, and I know it would only get worse. We decided to retire it from using big engines. I eventually sold the Minimax to a friend for $3. He intended to repair it as best he could and use a 3 hp Evinrude on it, with no plans to go with anything larger.

As I look back, that spring and summer were among my most memorable due to our Minimax adventures. Even though we pretty much destroyed the boat, and we knew full well what would most likely happen by using a motor rated at more than twice the recommended horsepower, we had the time of our lives and I'm just thankful we didn't destroy ourselves (or Kurt's father's Lark!) in the process.

THE INFLUENCE OF THE GREAT SOUTH BAY

CLAMS, SNAPPERS, CRABS AND SOFTIES

by Steven Naimoli

Summers in Amityville were full of adventures. We lived on the Amityville River at 9 Bourdette Place just off Ocean Avenue. My parents bought their house from the Wheeler family. The Wheelers were connected to the Wheeler Ship-building Company in Brooklyn. Ernest Hemingway's famous boat *PILAR* was a Wheeler—a 1934, thirty-eight-foot fishing boat.

As far back as I can remember my summers were spent crabbing and fishing. My father lived to fish. At an early age, he taught me crabbing and snapper fishing. I was hooked—no pun intended. He taught me to walk up and down the wood bulkheads and spot crabs hanging out, dining on the algae growing on the bulkheads. He showed me how to very gently lower the crab net into the water and to very quietly pull the net closer and closer to the crab and then swoop it in and catch the crab in the net.

Eating the crabs was just as enjoyable. I would boil them up, take them outside, sit on the dock with my legs dangling over the dock and feast away, throwing the "bones" into the river.

I think I had my first boat around eight years old. A small eight-foot dinghy with a three horsepower Evinrude outboard motor. That little boat went like a bat out of hell. Of course, it probably didn't go faster than five mph but to me I was doing 90.

After two or three years, I graduated to a larger boat, maybe 12 feet. As soon as I woke up, I went out to the dock and looked for crabs. I also loved casting for snappers—baby bluefish. On a light tackle spinning rod, you thought you had a five-pound striper on instead of a ten-inch snapper. But I didn't care!

Cleaning snappers was easy. You put your index finger through one gill and pushed it out the other gill. Then you pulled until the skin broke. Then you put your index finger down its gut and pulled. It ripped all of the guts out in one fell swoop and the fish was totally gutted. A frying pan, butter the pan, light salt and pepper and fry until the skin was a golden crisp—not too much—and they were the most tasty fish you can imagine. No fancy sauces—just sauté in butter, salt and pepper.

After I made my first walk along the dock, I got in my boat and checked out all the neighbor's docks looking for more crab. I couldn't get enough. I would catch one crab after another and just threw them in the bottom of the open boat. Pretty soon, most of the bottom was covered with crab. When I had enough, I headed home ready to cook them.

I would take one of my father's large spaghetti pots, fill it ¾ with water and bring it to a boil. Then I put the crabs in for maybe 15 or 20 minutes. One time, I poured out the boiling water toward me instead of away. The boiling water went all over my chest. I went to the hospital where they treated me for 3rd degree burns. I went home and ate the crab.

I would have crab and snapper for breakfast just about every day.

There was a small island in the middle of the Amityville River, just east of our house and I think right across from the Robinson's house. As kids, we went to the island a lot and played. My father discovered piss clams there. Ipswich clams—not regular littlenecks. We would go at low tide and we would see little holes where the clam pissed up that left this little hole. We would put our fingers as far down into the sand as possible and then scoop up a large amount of sand. In the middle would be a bunch of these clams. We would take them home, put them in a bushel basket and hang it over the dock, in the water, overnight. The clams would flush out all the sand. Then we would boil them up and serve with melted butter. Absolutely amazing.

My next adventure was soft shell crab. Eventually my father taught me about soft shell crabs or softies as we called them. All crustaceans shed their hard shells and that's how they grow. The hard shell would separate in the rear and the crab would literally back out of its shell, claws and all. When the crab emerged, it was 100% soft. Hardening started within a few hours. My father showed me how to pinch the shell under its left and right point. If it easily cracked, you knew it was going to shed. So, I checked each hard-shell crab I caught and found a bunch that were going to shed. I put them in a killie trap and waited for them to shed. I would check them every few hours and as soon as they shed, I took them out and had the best and fresh soft-shell crab. One of first times I did this, I had more than one shedder in the box at once. Well, when the crab shed and became soft, the other crabs ate it. All I found was the empty shell. I learned my lesson and made a larger box with screened compartments!

Cooking softies was similar to snappers. First you had to clean them. You cut off the mouth and eyes in the front. Pull up each pointed end and remove the gills and then remove the flap from the bottom of the crab. Again—sauté, salt and pepper and that's it. Again, no fancy sauces—nothing to diminish the wonderful and amazing taste of the soft shell crab.

The little island eroded away many years ago.

I continued this ritual every summer until I flew the nest. It is an amazing memory that will remain with me for the rest of my life.

The Influence of the Great South Bay

THE CRAB SANCTUARY

by Betty Robinson Zion

Amityville, its sparkling river, and the Great South Bay, provided the endless summers of childhood. Though it was our family home only until 1966, the year I turned twelve, it is where my deepest, warmest memories still take me.

Our house stood at the edge of the Amityville River, where folks waved as they motored past in boats of all sizes. The three islands that once existed in the river provided a great destination for playing pirates. Sunny docks stretched the length of the river and made for easy fishing and crabbing. There was always a boat tied up at our dock, of one type or another; our small cabin cruiser, the *Salt Shaker*, a Blue Jay sailboat, or my mom's very own *Tuesday's Child*, which my dad aptly named since her name was Grace—Monday's child is fair of face, Tuesday's child is full of Grace. Brothers Bob, Doug, and Glenn were the real sailors of the family and often raced on the Great South Bay.

In the early years, swimming at the Yacht Club was in the clear water of the bay. The Olympic size pool was later added and was a great boost for our swim team. The Yacht Club was a quick bike ride down Ocean Avenue, with a towel wrapped around my neck, and all the freedom and exhilaration of youth. Countless days of swimming and diving and the smell of French fries from the snack bar were the best!

Younger neighbor friends, Daphne and Debbie Ireland, once invited me on a boat outing with their grandmother, Grandma Dot. Grandma Dot was a petite and stylish lady with tanned legs and pretty lipstick. She had a small boat with an outboard motor and called it "Putt Putt." This, I knew, would be an adventure. I hopped aboard. We headed out the river and into the choppy bay. I recognized the channel markers as we made our way across the bay, to where flat, sandy islands ran parallel on our port side. The chain of islands was thick with the greens and browns of reeds and tall grasses. Grandma Dot pointed the bow straight for the dense reeds where we could see a small opening, just wide enough for the boat to glide through. The motor was pulled up, and a minute later we entered an enormous, shallow, saltwater sanctuary. Like ancient explorers, I was convinced this natural pond of water, surrounded on all sides by the islands, had never before been seen. The crystal clear water was knee-deep and the sandy bottom was covered with hundreds and hundreds of crabs. We floated, silently, in awe. Grandma Dot handed out long handled crab nets and large canvas totes. Not a word spoken, and careful not to cast a shadow, we scooped our nets full of crabs and dumped them into the totes. We hit the crab lottery and I was insane with excitement!

We gently floated wherever the boat took us, for more and still more crabs. The totes were laden with our catch. One of the totes fell over and spilled out crabs with angry claws and sent us shrieking, then laughing, and standing on the seats. With no more space to store the crabs, we called it a day.

Late in the day, the wind high, I sat in the bow as we headed for home. The expanse of water and sky was mesmerizing. The horizon was filled with unusual pinks and purples, all on fire, and I thought to myself: I will never forget this day, the best day, and I never have.

The slapping of the river and the rigging on the mast are the lulling evening sounds I recall from my bedroom window; feeling safely tucked-in after the fullness of the day.

So many adventures along the waterfront, Amityville was a great place to call home.

MEMORIES OF AMITYVILLE

by Carol Nehring

We lived on a canal; the Great South Bay was practically our back yard and figures large in my memories.

The summers were all about being out on a boat: a cabin cruiser, a sail boat, a row boat. Our first boats were a small cabin cruiser, the *Mardick*, and a row boat, the *Ott*. The *Ott* was fun to fool around in on the canal. We learned to row and would take it down to the bridge that crossed the canal. Here we would wait underneath in the cool darkness until a car rumbled overhead. Eerie, fun, the noise, the darkness: it was something we did. We would spend weekends on the *Mardick*: at West Gilgo, Hemlock Heading, the Coast Guard Cut. We'd head over to the ocean: build sand castles, sun, and swim.

One vivid memory. We were swimming in the ocean on a pretty rough day. I was trying to get back to the beach, but was hindered by the undertow. I looked over my shoulder to see a wave about to cascade over me. I turned to dive into the wave but instead was caught by it. I opened my eyes underwater, saw the sand swirling all around me, and felt that I was being buried alive. When the wave receded, my father was standing over me smiling. He helped me out of the water. Though scary, that smile made me feel less afraid. I still love swimming in the ocean and catching those waves that bring you ashore.

Other boats followed the *Mardick*: the *Skimmer*, the *Polaris*, the *Sandpiper* and the *Sanderling*. There was also a Blue Jay, the *Teal*, and a Seaford Skiff, the *Mudhen*.

My sister, Ginger, and I had learned to sail and raced the *Teal* most weekends. Our family, along with the Van Nostrands and Kennedys would head out to race week each year. We would race at the various yacht clubs up and down the Great South Bay. Following race week we would spend a week cruising, heading for coves and harbors on the bay and Long Island Sound. At our anchorages, the kids would get in the small boats and race to shore, renaming the various coves and beaches with the name of whoever stepped ashore first.

At some point my father wanted a sail boat. Our first sloop was the *Sandpiper*. Not quite as comfortable as the *Polaris*; the boat did not have headroom, and slept four. To accommodate our family of six, my father rigged pipe bunks over the mid-ship bunks. I was on an upper berth and every time my sister turned in her sleep, I would get a shoulder. We sailed the *Sandpiper* in the Cruising Club races. In one race, my father realized that the tide was running very strong against us and sent my sister forward to secretly lower the anchor. Pretty soon we were way ahead of the rest of the boats. When the tide started to slow down, we raised the anchor and sailed to the finish line, winning the race.

In the late Summer, Fall, we would head over to Hemlock Heading and the beach plum bushes. We'd pick buckets of the fruit and then spend days making beach plum jelly, a reminder in the winter of our summer fun.

A school memory includes my friend Cele Husing. I was the goody two-shoes and Cele was the more free spirit. She had gotten into trouble for wearing a dress that was a tad too short (not touching the floor when one knelt). We thought it would be interesting to see if I could wear the same dress and NOT get into trouble. Unfortunately, we had a dress assembly the very morning of our experiment, advising the boys not to wear their pants too tight and the girls not to wear their skirts too short. Upon leaving the assembly, one of the teachers started yelling and pointing at me, "And that is what we are talking about," and sent me to the principal's office.

Years later, I, with some friends, organized our class's 50th reunion. We had help from Bernie Goldberg, who had organized several previous reunions. He suggested that we probably needed more time to get the word out, so we had it a year later and included the class behind ours. We followed Bernie's plan; having events Friday, Saturday and Sunday. It was such an incredible experience to go back to the school for breakfast and a tour on Saturday morning then go to the Amityville Beach for a barbecue that afternoon. We danced to the music of Tony Tarantino's band (a classmate from the year ahead of us) and also of Leon Ognibene (our own classmate) at the dinner/dance Saturday evening. It was so good to get back in touch with so many old friends. A number of us have continued to see each other in following years. There is nothing like old friends.

THE INFLUENCE OF THE GREAT SOUTH BAY

THE DUCK BOAT

by Steven Bogan

The alarm rang at 5:15 a.m., and a weary arm reached out from under the covers to shut it off. Not just to wake himself, but to avoid waking others. Daybreak was still more than an hour away, but waterfowl wait for no man.

Billy rose and dressed warmly...cold on land is frigid on the bay. There was no UnderArmour back then, only long johns, thermal socks (multiple pairs) and sweaters under a drab green coat to form an outer shell that keeps heat in. It was tough to move around with all of those layers, but once in position, movement was the enemy.

The decoys were already loaded in the boat—only the gas tank and the gun bag had to be brought from the shed. At that time of day, the only sound was from the engine of another duck boat a canal or two over. The old Evinrude 9.9 started on the third pull, lines were cast off, and the slow trek to the mouth of the canal began. The trip seemed quicker this time of year. Most boats had been pulled for the winter by that point, so the 5 mph "No Wake" signs seemed more like a suggestion than a rule. There were no boats around to suffer damage, and, at this time of day, no glaring eyes to shame you into obedience.

Upon reaching the bay, it was time to open her up. To keep the boat in better balance and up on a plane, Billy stood forward and controlled the speed with an extension rod. Much more effective than sitting aft by the motor, but he missed the feel of the grip on the motor. The ride was much better with his weight forward, and the view spectacular.

The water was like glass, with no wind to cause a stir. Forget about whitecaps, there was barely a ripple on the Great South Bay this morning. The only motion was from the wake of other hunters moving out to the salt marsh. A perfect day, but less than a handful were out this morning. Billy heard stories from his dad, his uncle and their friends about hunting when they were boys—it seemed as if the bay must have been packed and finding a spot that was out of range from other shooters' gunfire must have been a challenge. But that was a long time ago. Today, there was plenty of room for everyone.

Duck boats don't require more than a few inches or so of water, so a more direct route across the bay could be used. The channel markers were still in place, guiding you past the Yacht Club to the mouth of the creek, before making the turn towards Sand Island and the Cross Bay Channel. In a larger boat of 30 feet or more, staying in the channel is the difference between fun on the water and a long day of waiting for the tide to roll back in and lift you off the sand bar. At barely 13 feet in length, the boat only needed the few inches that the outboard would need for the propellor to spin freely. Once Billy reached the marsh and was preparing to set the decoys, the motor would be turned off, the engine tilted up, and he could float in as little as three inches of water.

Setting the decoys was the art of the game, and separated the masters from the rookies. What would look natural to a duck, flying above in formation and looking for a good spot to take a break. Bunched? In formation? Random? Damned if I know, Billy thought to himself. He set them upwind from where he planned to sit and wait, in a modified "V" formation, and then drifted back to a little trench that was cut into the marsh. By bringing the boat in tightly and wedging it into the cut, it became part of the landscape. From there, it was time to settle in and wait for the ducks to fly at dawn.

All alone out there, with too little sleep but too cold to have trouble staying awake, a person can learn a lot about themselves. The mind is an interesting place—sometimes dark, sometimes creative, sometimes inventive, and sometimes full of shit. Sometimes all of these at the same time, or at least within minutes of each other. The serenity of the moment, peaceful, with the glow of the sunrise soon to come and the smell of salt marsh funk, always brought Billy to a state where he did his best introspective thinking. Truth be told, this is what he liked best about duck hunting. Different days brought different thoughts—school, sports, girls; past, present, future; who am I, who should I be, who will I be? Some days the mind was manic, jumping from thought to thought with no definable pattern other than the speed at which they came. Today, the canvas of the mind was more blank. Billy was a little zoned out, as if he was in a trance brought about by the calm of the moment. As the sun began to rise, he was in a state of total relaxation.

Just then, up to the left, about a dozen Brant were coming in. Flying low, would they land out of range, or keep coming? Stay still…wait it out…patience… patience… As they got to about 25 yards away, they started to pull up, exposing their breasts as their wingspans acted as brakes. It seemed like time slowed to a crawl, but it was in truth probably just a few seconds. Billy bolted upright, shotgun cocked and ready, and locked in on the grayish-black breast of one incoming bird…

WALKING ON WATER

by Kurt Nezbeda

Water is an interesting substance. Split into hydrogen and oxygen, both elements then chilled and liquefied, it powers rockets. It's the only material that expands when cooled to freezing. If you've ever had an engine block crack in winter, you know. That's why you add antifreeze.

Fresh water freezes at 32 degrees Fahrenheit. Salt water a tad above 28. NOAA tells us that when seawater freezes the ice contains very little salt because only the water part freezes. It can be melted and drunk. Who knew? Less dense, ice floats. If it sank, succeeding layers would solidly freeze any body of water.

The winter of 1962 was abnormally cold. Some of us saw a seal in the mouth of the Amityville River. Ice began to form early on the River and the other creeks in town. By the middle of January, those of us who gunned the Bay had to break ice in the boat slip to get to open water and the ducking grounds. Sitting in a duck boat in a quiet cove, we could see the surface of the water develop tiny vertical crystals. One could literally watch as the crystals coalesced and within minutes window pane ice would form. So called because it was thin, hard, and made a sound like breaking glass when struck with a paddle.

Duck season closed around the third week of January. It got colder. Much colder. Old timers told us that during the Depression the Bay occasionally froze. They claimed thick enough to drives cars on it. Light cars. Model Ts and As. But then those same guys told us they had to walk five miles to school...in the snow...

up hill in each direction.

The Bay froze. Solid. All the way across to Sand Island and as far as we could see toward West Gilgo. Three "Bay Ratz": Bruce Edwards, we think Stu Saxton, and I decided to take a walk after school. Stu has since gone to The Great Duck Blind in the Sky and can't confirm, or deny, this story.

We stepped off my folk's boat ramp onto the frozen Amityville River. It was a gray afternoon. Overcast, windless, and really cold. For some reason Bruce brought along my bike.

The river ice was relatively smooth. As we walked south past the Ocean/ Richmond Avenue public dock the surface became pebbly. Bruce got off the bike. Onto the open Bay the surface became even more corrugated.

The Bay at Amityville flows and ebbs the tides through both Fire Island Inlet to the east, and Jones Inlet the west. The tidal range is generally about 18 inches. That's a huge volume of water. The confluence of those tides apparently met along a north-south line just east of Unqua Yacht Club. Millions of tons of inexorable tidal pressure pushed two sheets of ice together. Edges locked, the opposing sheets rose to form a pressure ridge as tall as a one-story house. Gray, rough and foreboding, it paralleled our course toward Sand Island. Wish we had brought a camera.

There was a partially sunken clam garvey off the beach at Sand Island. About 16 feet in length, without motor or cabin, and devoid of clamming equipment, it was a spooky sight. A partially filled burlap bag of clams in the bilge was frozen into the ice's embrace. We could not break it free. We wondered where it had come from or what would become of it when the ice left. We never found out.

The Cross Bay Channel runs south from Sand Island to intersect the State Boat Channel and then into the West Gilgo Basin. Channel markers there were essentially telephone poles with white coned tops and steel arrow head points. The arrow heads point inward toward the channel. Someone had fired a rifle at a few of those arrow heads. Apparently military surplus ammo will shoot through steel. It wasn't any of us.

Ice will freeze around the rough surface of those poles. When the tide rises, the poles will be pulled s..l..o..w..l..y upward against the suction of the sand or mud below. As the poles rise the sand will fill underneath and prevent the poles from returning as the tide falls. As we walked down the channel we could see the poles tilted at crazy cockeyed angles to the left and right of us. In the spring someone would water jet those poles back into position.

The east- west State Boat Channel was frozen. Dredged in years gone by, it was deep and frequently white capped. Now frozen over. Solidly. The first time any of us had seen it that way.

Across to West Gilgo Basin. We walked along the east side of the cove. Home to a bed of soft-shelled clams. Steamers or "Piss clams," so named because their snorkels squirt water at low tide. Now under thick ice. Awaiting the spring and our clam rakes. Utter quiet. Not a sound or breath of air. Past the drunken poles of Unqua's "heading" dockage. No one in sight. Strangely surreal. Beautiful.

Darkness comes early in Late January. It's getting much colder. Time to hustle home.

THE INFLUENCE OF THE GREAT SOUTH BAY

LOOKING BACK

by Kim Ireland

Looking back at growing up in Amityville in the '40s and '50s, meant connecting with nature by boating on Great South Bay, ice skating on the canals, and having an active sports life with good friends in High School.

Being a small close knit community meant walking downtown to the movies, stores, or Avon lake to go fishing on opening day.

And of course, sailboat racing on Great South Bay was the highlight of many summers. The prevailing westerlies rolled in daily between noon to one p.m., providing ideal 15-knot breezes for sailing. Races lasted typically three hours over a triangular course where you got to hone your skills on all points of sail, from tacking to windward to reaching before the wind.

Approaching the starting line of the race to cross the line just as the starting gun went off was always fun, challenging and a little nerve-racking. Going over the line before the gun went off meant starting over while the rest of the fleet left you in the dust. Starting late meant the leaders had clean air and pulled out to a substantial lead right away.

Swimming at West Gilgo beach was a highlight of many a summer day. Body surfing was a favorite pastime as was barbecue at the dock.

School Days

SCHOOL DAYS

SCHOOL DAYS

SCHOOL DAZE...

by Howard DeNardo

It all started in September of 1959. It was my first day of Kindergarten in the Amityville Union Free School District. It started and ended rather quickly. My mom dressed me and walked me around the corner to Northwest School. She introduced me to my new teacher, Mrs. Guinn, sat me down and said goodbye. Mistake number one, goodbye?? As fast as mom exited the classroom door, I exited the classroom window, and was sitting on our front stoop when she got home.

I finally succumbed to my fears and began my daily school pilgrimage with my next door neighbor's children, who also attended the school. This was an era when everyone walked to school in groups. Parents didn't drive you to school or wait with you at bus stops. You were like the migration in Africa. You traveled in herds to find your source of water, aka school. It was pretty funny actually. You had groups traveling to three elementary schools, one junior high school and one high school. Crossing the rivers called County Line Road, Albany Ave, Route 110, and Merrick Road to safely arrive at their destination. But I am digressing a bit, more on that later.

Though I haven't been to Northwest in over fifty years, I still remember it like yesterday and, yes, I can still remember yesterday. It was shaped like a big U.

School Days

The front side of the U was the main entrance, main office, principal's office, kitchen, cafeteria, auditorium, and first and second grade classrooms. All classrooms on either side of the hallway had windows on one side. The bottom of the U had the kindergarten classrooms, special education, faculty lounge, nurse's office, gym and locker rooms. The back side of the U had classrooms for grades three to five.

The outside grounds were massive. Two baseball fields, a basketball court, handball court, and kindergarten playground were just part of the huge outdoor property. I would be remiss if I didn't mention a popular piece of the landscape that was part of the school septic system. The little cinder block structure that was affectionately called "The Stink House." Everyone remembers that place.

Northwest held a lot of memories for me. It is where I met most of my oldest childhood friends. It was my first indoctrination to team sports even though it was kickball. Our Boy Scout and Girl Scout meetings were held there. My first kiss was there as was my first fight. They might have been simultaneous...only kidding. My musical career began here as well. I tried playing the trumpet in the band but, being asthmatic, it was not the best choice and quickly ended. Things I remember most about my school days at Northwest are from a wide range. I remember our school crossing guard, Mr. Rice, in his uniform keeping us safe every day. He lived on the corner of Joyce Avenue and County Line Road right next to the school. I remember seeing my teacher, Mrs. Wilde, cry the day they announced over the public address system that President Kennedy was shot. There was a crazy activity that we participated in called air raid drills. I remember Mrs. Kellogg introducing us to the world of reading and books. Thank you, Mrs. K. There was show and tell time. It's funny the things you remember but there was a time a classmate had a father who was a butcher. He brought in a chicken foot and worked the tendons so it appeared to be some bizarre marionette. That always amazed me in a crazy sort out way. And then came fifth grade.

Mr. Otto Behensky was a fabulous teacher that I'll never forget. He made you work and play hard. His tactics would not work today in a day of non-disciplinary education . He would stand in front of you with his arms holding the side of your desk. He would look you in the eye when asking you a question and If you didn't give him the right answer he would head-butt you. I think I have a permanent calcium deposit on my forehead from those days. Pretty tough on a small fifth grader. But he would reward you too. You would be working on an assignment and you would look up and on the blackboard and there would be the word "kickball," or "scooter," and it would be a mad dash to the gym. We all loved those moments. Never will I forget those times and the work ethic it installed in me.

Other than my Dad, Mr. Behensky was my biggest influence into enjoying the game of football. He was a Syracuse grad and would test you on the results of Orangemen football games. These games were usually telecast on WPIX 11. Those years Syracuse was a national power. They were led by two players whose careers I followed into the old AFL days. They were Hall of Famer Floyd Little of the Denver Broncos and Jim Nance of the Boston Patriots. I still watch and root for Syracuse to this day.

One other thing I always remember is that he encouraged our class to create a yearbook. Everyone was organized into committees just like a High School yearbook. We worked the entire school year on this project. It was so much fun and I still have a copy to this day. The best part was that our photo was a comic book character decided on by your classmates. Mine was the Flash. This was not because of foot speed, but the speed I answered his questions. Hence, my calcium deposit! Thank you Otto Behensky.

The next phase I call "reality check" time. There were three kingdoms in Amityville. They were called Northwest, Northeast, and Park Avenue. They are the three elementary schools that funneled into the new Junior High School. They were three distinct entities. Northwest was predominantly white. Northeast was black and Park Avenue consisted mostly of Amityville Village proper residents. Our worlds collided when we entered the Junior High School. The Junior High consisted of sixth grade, which was classroom format, then grades seven through nine where you had a home room and scheduled classes.

It was tough skating at first because it is by nature that you stay with your group. A lot of us were never exposed to having blacks in our class so this was truly unique. It was a learning curve. I will never forget my first day there. Seeing kids bussed in was also new to me. It was my first trek across County Line Road and Route 110 via Maple Drive. It would be my route for the next four years. The assimilation of our little kingdoms took about two years. The first year was tough because we were still kind of grouped in classroom formats. The second year, when we became free range, is when it truly started. I have to be honest, it was hard. April 4th 1968, didn't make it any easier. That was the day Martin Luther King Jr. was assassinated. Racial tensions stirred and school had to be closed. We were pawns in the games of our parents. What did we know about the civil rights movement before this. I believe the aftermath made us stronger as a class. Some times there were fights, some times there were laughs. But eventually the laughs and smiles won.

Freshman sports started here, setting the foundations for future varsity teams. I so looked forward to those teams. As a kid I remember watching teenagers get off their buses and crossing the Northwest playground wearing their football jackets with the big "A" on them. When my freshman football season came, it was very promising. After relinquishing my dream of becoming a running back because I blocked too well, I became the worlds smallest lineman. I played both ways as an offensive and defensive guard. I had a great first game but then the next week, injury happened. During a pileup my leg was locked behind me and I broke my ankle. It was bad; it was on my growth plate and I was in a cast for 4 months. It still bothers me today. The Doctors told me not to play football again. I was heartbroken. But once again I fooled them as my growth spurt was over. I never grew up, just out. It was a lost year as I could not play any other sports and I was home-schooled for four months. I will never forget the friendships I made, some that are still growing strong during these years. And every day on the way home there was a stop at Keg Beer for a 25¢ Black Cherry or Cola soda.

Next stop was High School. Now I entered new territory as a member of the sophomore class. Just when you thought you were king of the hill, you were now back at the bottom. To me, it was like "Land of the Giants." These were grown up people. Girls became beautiful young women who I lost sleep over. Boys became men and big men at that. Despite what you hear about teachers today, some of the best influences of the man I am today came from them. The best of which was Edmund Miles. He didn't just teach, he mentored. That is why the Junior High bears his name today. You had to excel in his classes. He prepared you for the future even though you hated it at the time. The easiest test of the year was the New York State Regents. Thank you for what you did, Mr. Miles. My love for history came from two great teachers, Ben Kurland and Norm Maisel. They made history fun to learn rather than just people and dates. It's funny, every day I am amazed at what I remember from these insightful men. There were crushes of the ladies, too many to name, during these years, too. And then there was football.

As I said earlier, I remember the guys cutting through the playground with their Tide jackets on, sporting their varsity letters. I so wanted to be a part of that. After breaking my ankle as a Freshman and told not to play again, I knew I had to. I used to go to the High School and watch practices waiting for my time to come... The tradition of Amityville Football and what it means is a book in its self. Great boys who became great men were a part of it. Learning the meaning of true sportsmanship and team work. For some, it was their last stand and others went on to future greatness on and off the gridiron. I remember hearing the names Dan Cutillo, Dan Scott, and Charlie Wilson while watching Ohio State and Michigan State games and beaming with pride. Watching the Super Bowl with Amityville's John Niland was incredible. Like I said, too many to name, it's another book.

The spring before my sophomore year I knew I had to be ready to play. I was small in stature but big in heart. One of my freshman coaches, Mr. Strong, told me he loved my desire and inspired me to try. I'd ride my bike 2 1/2 miles to get to the High School for "Two-a-Days." If I was lucky, I was able to catch a ride.

I remember taking a tradition test about all the players who played before me in order to get a uniform. There were great names: Kretz, McDonough, Leftenant, Davis, and Cutillo to name a few. And of course all the "#31s," a number presented to the best back by a team vote every year. It was great way of keeping traditions alive as well as the memory of these great players. You had to have a perfect score.

You had to endure the coaches and all their drills; Bull in the Ring, Up-Down, Oklahoma's, The Sled, Wind Sprints, and Running Tires. Vic Niemi and Norm Maisel were relentless in preparing us physically and mentally. Water on the field was a privilege. We were always so gassed. I remember as a sophomore, walking out and seeing the size of some of the returning players and saying to my self, just do your best. Don't show them you're afraid.

Then there was the Red/Gray game and its "bar of soap" admission to see who would make the team. Yes, cuts back them. When you made it your dream had become reality. You got your Tide jacket. You had to wear a black sweater and white shirt to school on Fridays before games. The first team defense was selected in a candle lit ceremony and given the title of Blackwatch, named after the Royal Military Scottish Regiment.

On game days we had a team breakfast made by the team moms and served by our beautiful cheerleaders. Then we attended religious services as a team. I remember the whole village in the stands watching us play. It was like the Packers in Green Bay, everyone came. Horns blaring as we entered the field. Little kids knew the players by name. It's was a place to see and be seen by your friends and classmates. And of course you parents and teammates parents were always there! Away games were no different. A caravan of cars would follow us to the games. There was always Pride in The Tide.

I remember all my teammates, some of the best athletes I ever saw to this day; some of the best friends and brothers you could ever have. Regardless of what was going on in the world around us, we were always brothers. Truly a tradition that should be brought back to the teams of today. As you can see, this was the joy of my high school years.

When graduation came it was a day well earned. I said goodbye to some classmates I would never see again but will always remember. Others continue to be a part of my life today. You can take the boy out of Amityville but you can't take Amityville out of the boy. Thanks to my teachers for building my character and knowledge. Thanks to all for the memories.

School Days

MEMORIES

by Maryann Ford

I moved to Amityville when I was four years old; we moved from South Ozone Park. We moved to 91 Bernard Street. The house we moved into was weird! The one bedroom had built in beds and drawers! Our bathroom was painted black. We would walk to Northwest Elementary, don't know how far it was, but I would say at least an hour to get there. I had Mrs. Quinn for Kindergarten; just loved her! First grade I had Mrs. Kramer, loved her too! Second grade, I had Mrs. Kellogg and loved her too. Third grade I believe I had Mrs. Zailor. I was only there for about a month then I got accepted into Our Lady of Lourdes in Massapequa Park.

At Christmastime a whole bunch of people would carol at each person's house. We would practice for a couple of weeks, then go caroling! We would have block parties on our block! We put up picnic tables on the road and block the streets so nobody might drive down while we were having our party. Fourth of July was big at our house. Dad and I would go to the fish market and buy huge amounts of clams and we had a big steamer to steam the clams! We had an octagon shaped pool with a redwood deck and we would swim all day. That night we had one of the biggest fireworks displays. All my uncles would travel somewhere out of state to buy them! We would ride our bikes to Bethpage State Park and pack our lunches. You could also rent a bicycle built for two! A bunch of us would play army; the guys would be the soldiers and the girls would be the nurses! So many fond memories!

School Days

SCROOGE

by Stephanie Deckert-Racanelli

I was four years old when Dad pulled out the Yellow Pages, searched for an address, and announced that we were heading to the Bideawee Animal Shelter.

We stood before the cages and looked at all of the sad faces. I had my eye on a scrappy little mutt, but dad tried to dissuade me. He wanted the trained Sheepdog. I wanted the sad little terrier/beagle mix.

We left with the light brown mutt, whom we promptly named Scrooge.

Over the years Scrooge constantly ran away from our home on Bennett Pl. There were times he did not return until the following morning. These were the days of no fencing, or the rustic Post and Plank type of fence, allowing dogs and people to roam the entire neighborhood via everyone's backyard (we would go from South Ireland Pl. to Prospect St. by cutting through front and back yards!) Scrooge roamed everywhere, helping himself to various items that he'd pick up in random porches and yards. We amassed a collection of stolen goods: shoes, gloves, hats, a hose, a lawn chair cushion, bags of bait, defrosting meat, and even a bag of bagels! He was a vagabond on four feet—occasionally spotted roaming miles from our home.

When Scrooge wasn't casing the neighborhood or chasing cars, he was following me to the bus stop or to school. In the years that I took a bus, he would make a mad dash from behind a tree, and run up the stairs, quickly wedging himself under the back seat. This was hysterical for all of the children on board, but highly stressful for me! I'd yank him out and deposit him on the corner of Grace Ct. and Ocean Ave., and watch him from my window as he ran behind the bus.

In the fourth grade I walked to Park Avenue School. On many mornings Scrooge would appear along side me and my friend, Jeanne Dooley, and ignore our pleas to GO BACK HOME!!! Each time we hollered at him, he would disappear for a minute, and reappear from behind another tree. One particular morning, he ran out in front of us just as we were opening the side door of the Park Central building. He bolted into the school, past our classroom and Mrs. Schlinger's office, and up the closest staircase. He proceeded to the second floor and ran in and out of the classrooms. By this time, we had a group of people chasing him. Mr. Grey, (the principal), Mr. Sullivan (my teacher), and several students chased him into Mr. Corrado's class, where Scrooge's escapade came to an end. The door was shut behind him. I had to scoop him up and carry him downstairs to call my parents on Mrs. Schlinger's phone. I was mortified! The students thought it was hysterical. My parents didn't believe me! They came to get him and we all carried on with our day.

Scrooge lived a long life, mellowing a bit in his old age. I will never forget my crazy mutt who endured dress-ups and being wheeled around in a baby pram. We speak about him often and never regret not taking the fully trained sheepdog home that day. Life was way more exciting with our little four footed vagabond...

HIGH SCHOOL MEMORIES

By Susie Falkenbach Welch

In the '50s and '60s, sports were extremely important to some of us, although the number of sports offered to us was quite limited. Interested girls tried out and they might be put on a class team or an honor team. This was several years before Title IX, and there were no varsity sports yet for the girls in Amityville. There were several levels of points to reward young women athletes for excellence and they were highly coveted—the rewards included numerals, shields, the Amityville letter A, and an invitation to join Leaders Club and wear a red blazer with an emblem. The most dedicated and athletic girls hoped to get enough points to get the highest athletic award for girls then, a Gold Key. We practiced, some of us got on the various teams, we got onto buses to go to other schools, and we played our hearts out. There were few if any spectators. I don't remember really caring about that since we knew we were playing for ourselves and our teammates and maybe for bragging rights. When we had a sports banquet, it was just the girls and the coaches.

Sportsnight was a major evening production sponsored by the Girls' Phys. Ed. Department and held for the whole community, usually annually. All the girls were on either the Red Team or the Grey Team, and each team had a theme and created a theme song as well. Team Captains were chosen, as well as lieutenants and it was quite an honor for the girls who led their teams. We worked with our teammates for weeks in gym classes and also after school, and we were all very secretive about

ELECTION WINNERS: Chosen at Amityville Memorial High School to lead the senior class in its final year are, left to right, Erica Donovan, chairman of the class council; Diane Brice, treasurer; Owen Bradford, president; Susan Falkenbach, secretary; and Gil D'Andrea, vice-president. Just through with a strenuous magazine campaign to raise class funds, the officers are now busy planning for their first social event of the year, a dance this weekend.

Our senior year officers for the AMHS class of '61.

what our team was doing. There were several different areas of competition such as the grand entrance, dancing, marching, acrobatics, calisthenics, and tumbling, and the grand finale, where each team was judged and given points. The costumes were all handcrafted. At the end of the evening, the winning team for each event was announced, and then the overall individual winner. Sportsnight was a big deal, very competitive, and brought out leadership skills and athletic abilities in the young women who participated. In the Sportsnight in March, 1958, I was in my freshman year. When I recently looked at the 1958 yearbook, I was reminded that the theme of the Red Team was "Space Bound," and the Grey Team was "Under the Big Top." I realized that I actually could still sing a part of the Red Team song: "How great, how witty, the red team is. We've flown our saucers and we're a whiz... Give me just a spot of, not a lot of grey, hey! Red Team will take it away." The song was sung by the whole team (it was to the tune of Thou Swell, a Rodgers and Hart song from a 1920s Broadway musical). Despite what the Red Team song said, though, the yearbook reminded me that it was the Grey Team that "took it away" in 1958. Oh, well.

We had many parties, including pajama parties for the girls. One especially memorable pajama party was in the big room above Whitenack's boathouse. There was a bunch of us girls who went, and it was in the summer, probably 1959. That night, we were the "victims" of a panty raid. Of course, that only happens when one or more of the girls lets one or more older boys know where the pajama party is and that there won't be supervision—no, it was not I who got the word out. A few boys ran up the stairs, noisily; we girls screamed a lot, and then the boys ran back down the stairs and disappeared. I'm quite sure none of the girls had any undergarments stolen, but it was still very exciting. Later that night, we decided to take a swim, and one of the girls tied her bathing suit to a buoy. Yes, she really did. When we came back (and, oh boy, I sure hope we swam with each other for safety on that moonless night), her suit was gone. I remember which girl that was, but I am not telling. If she were to read this, she would remember. We were all quite modest in those years, and I don't remember how she got out of the water without her suit; but I know that if it had been me, I would have remembered that!

Another pajama party was at Brice's house, and I think we slept on their porch. The Brices also let DeeDee have at least one boy-girl party (not, of course, a pajama party) in the barn when we were in junior high, and we played the usual game of spin the bottle. When the bottle made the decision, the fated couple went into a little room inside the barn, almost like an indoor shed. In the mid-1950s, playing spin the bottle was an acceptable way to practice our kissing skills.

One of the many very special people in our class was Roddy McBrien. He was very musical all through school and was voted Best Musician by the seniors in 1961. He continued after high school as a professional musician and eventually owned his own production company in NYC. He was a well-known success in advertising music and a four-time Clio Award winner for his work for Coca-Cola and other national advertisers. Some of his recognizable tunes are "Have It Your Way" (Burger King), "Soup Is Good Food" (Campbell's), "Look Up America" (Coca-Cola), "Who Wears Short Shorts" (Nair; Clio winner), "If You've Got the Time, We've Got the Beer" (Miller Beer). He was also honored in Washington DC where he was recognized in Congress for the songs he had written for America's Veterans. He had a knack for keeping in touch with a number of Amityville school friends, and I was one of the lucky ones. He and I stayed in touch until his untimely and unexpected death in 2009 from complications from surgery.

SPORTS IN AMITYVILLE

Sports in Amityville

CARDBOARD GOLD

by Howard DeNardo

I remember watching the 1962 World Series with my dad and I think that was my first introduction to Yankee baseball. Ralph Terry pitching a complete game with Bobby Richardson grabbing a Willie McCovey smash to give the Yankees the Championship. I was eight years old and wanted to play baseball.

My favorite player was, of course, Mickey Mantle, who I idolized. It was a shame I never got to see him in his prime. I remember my Uncle Stanley taking me to games and watching him take batting practice. I was in awe!! Just walking down the Grand Concourse and seeing the frieze of the Stadium would send chills down my spine. Sitting in the bleachers watching the Yankees was a dream come true. And catching a ball was the ultimate reward. Still have a few from back then. In 1965, the Yankees had their first bat day. They didn't have a great team then as they finished eighth with an aging team. I was lucky to go and got a Ross Moschitto bat. Who???

My Grandfather, Rocco, helped me get my first Mickey Mantle glove by saving the bands from his Phillies cigars and I always wore number seven in Little League. Even as a young man playing softball, I still wore number seven.

Growing up in the 1960s, baseball was going through an amazing era. It was a time when a new National League team called the New York Mets was born and loved by our parents who loved the Giants and the Dodgers before they moved to the west coast. They had Casey Stengel as their first Manager and old stars like Duke Snider and Gil Hodges. Everybody loved the Mets. That season, of course, they were the darlings of baseball and set a record for futility losing 120 games. Baseball had stars like Clemente, Koufax, Spahn, Robinson, Mays, Aaron, Mathews, and Maris, to name a few, that were household names and legends of the game. The players of this era were not the millionaires of today. They didn't live in mansions in their own little elite world. They lived among us and most had second jobs to support their families. As a boy, I delivered the Long Island Press to Dennis Ribant and Larry Bernarth. They were both pitchers for the Mets and resided in Frontier City Trailer Park in Amityville. Met stars, Ron Swoboda and Ed Kranepool also lived close by and owned the DugOut Restaurant on Broadway.

Every young boy wanted to play baseball at some level. We started playing in the streets of our neighborhood and school yards. Eventually we all became members of the Amityville Little League. We had great teams with sponsors some will remember like perennial champion Mole Ford, Franklin National Bank, Evans Dairy, and Security National Bank. There were three fields in Amityville to go along with three levels of play. The A field was our Yankee stadium and top players played there. It was a dream to hit a homer over the fence on the A field. It was located on Louden Avenue. The B field was on County Line Road and was also a beautiful field to play on. The C fields were at Northwest School. This was the starting point for the younger players. We all wore our different colored team caps with the Big A on it to designate what team we were on, everywhere we went. Baseball was definitely king in the '60s. It's hard to believe that with all the great players that played on those fields, none ever made it to the major leagues. It just goes to show you how hard it was to play baseball at that level back then. I can only think of one player, Kenny Young, who played in the Red Sox system in the late seventies, who got close.

As young fans of the game, we all also became traders in a commodity called

cardboard gold—baseball cards. All of us would be wealthy men if we just held on to our assets to this day. Back in the fifties and sixties collecting baseball cards was a hobby for children. Cards, comic books, Famous Monsters and Mad magazines were our video games. It was a shame that greed destroyed the hobby.

The year was 1963. I was first introduced to them by my next door neighbor, Jim Carrol. We went to his friend's house on Emily Street where there was a group of boys flipping through stacks of these beautiful photographed images of all the legends I had seen on television. They were performing a strange chant that went like this. "Got 'em, Got 'em, Got 'em, Need 'em." When the need was there the trades began. Al Kaline would command a trade of three or four lesser players. Willie Mays could cost you a dozen or more cards. I was hooked.

I asked my Mom for twenty five cents and jumped on my bike to Woolworth's at Intercounty Shopping Center. There were a lot of bikes out front as the word on the street was that the Series Three of Topps 1963 set was out. Topps was smart back then. They released their cards in seven to eight series during the baseball season. Every series release brought on these mass exoduses. I bought five wax packs of baseball cards which also came with the worst stick of gum you ever tasted. You looked like a bizarre hamster stuffing these slabs of gum into your mouth as you opened your packs. Pack #2 produced my first Yankee, Ralph Houk. I loved the

Yankee Logo that was on his card as manager of the New York Yankees. Pack #5 I'll never forget. In this pack lodged between The Cubs team and Joe Christopher of the Mets was The Mick.....I couldn't believe my eyes. I had my first Mickey Mantle card in my hand. Neither could the other boys. It was like being a trader on the floor of the New York Stock Exchange. I was circled and all offers were being shouted to me. I took none. I have this card to this day.

This was just the beginning. I began to comb the fields and the woods around Northwest School and South Oaks Hospital for discarded deposit bottles to cash in to grow my collection. Most stores back then would sell out of wax packs. You had to search where they would be available. Usually the amount of bikes out front was the give away. My stores of choice were Woolworths, The Luncheonette, and Ellis Stationery in Intercounty Shopping Center. Next stop would be Lakes Luncheonette on Broadway. My last resort was my farthest ride. I was gone with the Schwinn to McClellans Department Store in town.

During these times, every wall represented a place where you would pitch your cards to see if you could get the closest to it. The winner would take the pot. If you got a card that leaned against the wall and someone knocked it down, that would get you one extra card from the players. There were other ways to increase your collection. You could flip your card and if it landed on the front or the back, you would tell your opponent to match it or not. If he didn't you would win his card. There was a game called "Teams." Each player would have his stack of cards randomly sorted. You would put a card down on a center pile until, for example, one player puts a Senator card down and the next player puts another Senator on top, he would win the pile. Another game was colors played the same way as Teams but using the card border colors. You could go to school or the Northwest handball court with ten cards and come back with a hundred. Of course the reverse was true. I remember card flipping champs that you stayed away from. Howie

Belgrod and Gary Bush come to mind.

A lot of kids used the cards to make their Stingrays sound like a Harley. They attached the cards to the spokes using clothes pins. Hard to believe the fortune in today's market that was lost doing this. They could be buying real Corvettes and Harley Davidsons.

Baseball was so much a part of our life back then. It was a game we shared with our friends and families. Passed down from parents to children. Baseball cards kept me out of trouble and I cherish the memories I shared with my friends collecting and trading them. Seeing our favorite stars playing at Shea or Yankee Stadium was affordable for a family. Not the high prices to support the salaries of today's players. You could get discount tickets off Borden's milk cartons and as a newspaper carrier, *Newsday* and the *Long Island Press* were rewarding us with them for new customers. It was an amazing time to love baseball and grow up in Amityville.

Sports in Amityville

OUR CHAMPIONSHIP SEASON: A VIEW FROM THE BENCH

by Peter Sittler, with help from Ed Weeks,
Weaver Miller, Eliot Bradford, and the late Ken Marsala

Being on a championship team will always be one of my fondest memories. Coach Jack Schmitt asked me to join his team in November, 1959. I had a growth spurt beginning over my sophomore/junior summer. I was 6′5″ by then and was dunking volleyballs during gym. I could not even dribble the ball, but was useful in practice trying to give Bill McCollough (four-year scholarship to Hofsta) some kind of competition. Believe me, there was none.

Ken Marsala was clearly the leader. He sent emails to some of us that are detailed below.

But it certainly was a very diverse team and everyone contributed. Ken Marsala, who passed away four years back, wrote the following about that season in an email to Ed Weeks in 2008, prior to our AMHS 50th reunion:

I got to Amityville the end of our sophomore year. Was friends with Wyatt's brother who idolized Bernie. The tradition of giving the number 31 to the high scoring football player was unique and a fun idea. I was more wrapped up with the 3 M's on the basketball team. What a great experience. Coach Schmidt saw me the first time in gym class. When I told him I played ball at the city school I attended, he gave me a basketball and in front of the whole class asked me to take a few shots at the basket. He was more excited than any coach ever was with my skills. Doug Hepburn was a terrific ballplayer and excellent dribbler. In our junior year, he was our team leader. He couldn't play with us our senior year due to his heart murmur.

Marsala, McCollough & Miller led our Amityville team to the Suffolk County Championship. Billy led the county in scoring, Weaver was our steady shooter and I helped getting them the ball and also played my best game in the championship game. With Earl Craig, John Lowe, Jim Gibb, Peter Sittler, Chuck Goehring, Larry Bourgard and Bruce Lottman each playing important roles and sophomores Skip Hepburn and Norm Sonne offering hope for the future, it was a good group of high school champions.

Ah, memories. Still smiling!

Ken

Ken had the following comments in an email he sent to Weaver Miller in 2008. Weaver's reply is included; kind of sweet, for Weaver:

Hi Weaver:

Without "Deadeye Weaver," I doubt we could have won the champi-onship in our senior year. You were our best shooter, both on the wing and on the foul line. You also pulled down your fair share of rebounds. Did you play any ball after HS? Enjoy all your e-mails. Stay healthy.

Ken talked to Laverne Norris she has Thomasina Thomas' address I forgot to get it i'll call her this weekend and get it for you Deadeye Weaver

Amityville High School's basketball squad, which is ent red in a Christmas tournament in Hauppauge, starting Monday. Back row, from left: Jack Schmitt, coach; Peter Sittler, Ken Marsalla, John owe, Bill McCollough and Norman Sonne; front: Jim Gibb, Larry Bourgard, Roland Hepburn, Weaer Miller and Earl Craig.

Ken's last email on basketball included the following reply to Eliot Bradford.

Hi Guys: Eliot sent in a class donation and a great letter with some
basketball memories that made my day. Goes to show you what a
boring life I have. This was the e-mail I sent him in reply to his letter.

Hi Eliot:

I got a kick reading of your flashback of our junior year on the basketball
court, especially the game against S. Huntington and Paul Lombardi.

"...I had a flashback to the last game of the '59 season against S. Huntington. Half the school had flu. Hepburn, Miller & McCollough all missed the game. You stood off the bad guys almost single handed, a junior who we in the stands hadn't previously paid much attention. You went one on one against Lombardi, their star and held your own."

He got the best of me that game but our duel was not yet over. I don't remember much about basketball in our junior year (my first at AMHS), only that we were all learning how to play together. What I do remember is my first day in gym class as a new sophomore (mid way thru the year). Coach gave me a basketball and told me to go out on the court and take some shots. (In front of the entire class) I laughed, had some fun and must have looked good. He said he wanted me to come out for the team.

I do remember Doug Hepburn's sad news about a heart murmur and not being able to play our senior year. My best game our championship season was against Paul Lombardi and S. Huntington. Sweet revenge! We each won one game during the season. Although we had one more game to play, this was the game to determine who was the favorite to win the county championship. The paper the next day had the coach's comments and you would have thought I could walk on water. "Marsala's the Star" was the headline and Jack asked if anyone ever saw anyone like that kid Marsala, whose ball handling skills... etc., etc, etc... Scored 18. We got the lead and I kept eating up the clock to keep Paul's team from catching up.

Of course, Weaver and Billy and a great supporting team were the main reasons we got to the county tournament and eventually won the Suffolk County Basketball Championship

Coach invited me to tag along with him and 4 county all-stars to Iona College to help them try for a basketball scholarship. Thought I had one to Providence College so I had no pressure on me during the scrimmage. I had a great scrimmage and Iona's coach offered me a full ride which I accepted. Dismal college career but I stayed and graduated.

Ken

Ken Marsala was special and we all miss him. He was an inspiration to many and well-loved by his family. He is buried in Arlington National Cemetery. While this book was being assembled we learned of Weaver Miller's passing. He will be missed.

I might be incorrect, but the only loss we had in 1959-60 was to South Huntington in a scrimmage game coach Schmidt arranged for us up in Huntington before the season started. We must have defeated them in that Christmas tournament, as Ken said that we had split two games. Although an unofficial game, there were two referees there, whistles and all. My father came out to the practice, all the way from New York City. He never saw me play another game until the championship, which I believe was played in South Huntington. Divorce crap had him living in Brooklyn.

The picture printed in the Amityville Record, December 24, 1959, had the following people: Coach Jack Schmitt, myself, Ken Marsala, John Lowe, Bill McCollough, Norman Sonne, Jim Gibb, Larry Bourgard, Roland Hepburn, Weaver Miller and Earl Craig. We were entered in a Christmas tournament (Hauppauge). We won that one and went undefeated to win the Suffolk County Championship. Up until then, it was Lou Howard's inspirational coaching combined with an ample supply of talented football players that produced many undefeated teams. I was lucky to be on that basketball team in that year. A bonus was—being on the bench for most of the game—-sitting next to the cheerleaders. However, I did not date in high school. But that's another story.

GAME DAY IN AMITYVILLE

by Bruce Chattman

The varsity football team began the day by congregating in the AMHS locker room at 8:00 in the morning. Upon arrival, we would place our freshly washed uniforms and game socks in our lockers. We would travel by carpool or foot (depending upon distance) to a place of worship. The place of worship would vary each week and included Protestant Churches, the Catholic Church and the Synagogue. While there, we were asked to quietly reflect upon our personal faith and to pray for our opponents as well as ourselves. We were guided to pray that we would play to the best of our ability, stay safe from injury and to be grateful for the opportunity before us; an opportunity to represent our families, friends and school with fairness, character and good sportsmanship. After this time for reflection, we were to report to the home of one of the players (this varied by week), where we were hosted by a group of proud moms and dads and served a delicious meal, high in protein and carbohydrates. Also in attendance at the breakfast were the members of the JV and Varsity Cheerleading Squads who diligently waited on us with smiles and good cheer. Needless to say, this was a very pleasant breakfast for everyone. There was no focus or expectation at the breakfast other than to relax, laugh and enjoy our camaraderie as only a large group of young men can do, where the presence of parents and young ladies on the cheer teams certainly provided an unstated forum for decorum and restraint.

Up until this juncture, there was no pep talk, no mention of the opposing team and no specific focus on the game yet to be played. All game-focused energy was reserved for after 11:00 when we were expected to be back in the locker room. Upon arrival in the locker room, we became all business and winning a football game became our sole, common, focus. Our first task was to polish, in silence, our black shoes using fresh polish and to insert new white laces. We would be led upstairs to the wrestling room by the team captain where we would spread out and sit on the mat to accomplish this task, while listening to college football fight songs blasted over the school speaker system. We were expected to keep a focus on our opponents and reflect upon how we would win the game and the consequences of losing—of which we were well-schooled all week by our post-practice reviews with Coach Howard.

At noon, we were to be back in the locker room where we would suit up in our uniforms, all the while still listening to football fight songs with our silence no longer required. The Captain and other team leaders would begin to challenge and increase the intensity of our energy and spirit for the entry into the combat of the game. We would then be led out to the practice field at 12:30 for warm up exercises where we would be once again joined by Coach Howard and his assistant coaches. About 1:15, we would return to the locker room where we sat and waited, still with the fight songs playing, until the music stopped. On this cue, it was time for Uncle Lou to enter the locker room and take us to the next level of mental and emotional preparation. He would reference and challenge us to do our best and make it personal for specific players based upon situations relevant to the game (e.g. derogatory media, personal attacks/quotes by other teams/coaches). He would remind us of our hard work and preparation, our school history of victories with our obligation to not fail, causing us to believe in ourselves and our ability to prevail. The man's mind and voice were naturally created to inspire. He spoke with passion, would pause strategically to let us absorb his words, and then would conclude with enthusiasm and a challenge to win. Lou's voice would rise in pitch naturally emphasizing his own emotions, excitement and challenges to us. He would then leave the locker room and leave us to rev up our own emotions and aggression.

When it was time to enter the field (and we were strategically always last to enter), we would gather outside the locker room entrance and walk silently to the entrance to the field. Because our locker room was on the opposite side of the high school from the entrance to the football field, the fans and pep band were unaware of our presence until we rounded the building and came into sight. Then the cheering commenced and the pep band played the school song. We would continue to walk to the entrance, forgoing our silence and beginning our own emotional build up while still walking, albeit at a faster place until we entered the gate. We were like racehorses, as we passed the gate and charged the field en masse at full speed with unbridled aggression and noise intended to intimidate our opposition.

Post game, we would again return to the locker room and be addressed by Uncle Lou. His tone was of a different mode whereby his pitch remained consistent as he praised and thanked us for our effort, gave acknowledgement to different players for things well done and tell us to celebrate responsibly and conclude by asking us to all take a knee to end the day as it began for us as a team—united for a few minutes of silence for personal reflection and prayer. When he said "Amen," we were free to shower and go home to our families and friends.

In 1990 the Amityville Football Field was dedicated to Lou Howard and in 1991, he was inducted into the Suffolk County Sports Hall of Fame. He never had a losing season, and won nine consecutive league championships, which has never been duplicated on Long Island. His teams won five consecutive Rutgers Trophies, given to the best team in Suffolk County, and he is the only coach to ever retire the trophy.

In addition to being a teacher of drivers' education and head football coach at AMHS from 1951 through 1966, Uncle Lou was also a vibrant member of the greater Amityville community and once owned the Amityville Record newspaper. Because of his immense popularity, he was often chosen to speak at community events, ride at the head of parades and attend weddings of former students. He served several terms as the Mayor of Amityville, was subsequently elected to the Suffolk County Legislature and ultimately elected as a Representative to the New York State Assembly. He also held a doctorate in Aerospace Technology, held a pilot's license, instituted and developed the Aerospace program at SUNY Farmingdale and is a member of the Farmingdale College Aviation Hall of Fame.

REMEMBERING
LOU HOWARD

REMEMBERING LOU HOWARD

EGGBEATER

by Kurt Nezbeda

It was the early '50s. Parents didn't helicopter. Baby Boomer boys, urchins, went exploring. They headed home only after hearing a neighbor's cowbell announcing the dinner hour.

The scrawny eight-year-old easily scaled the chain link fence at the northeast corner of the practice field. The football team was on that field every school day afternoon in the Fall.

Amityville was on the cusp of becoming the powerhouse football team on Long Island. Lou Howard, with his trademark white cap, was its coach. "Lou" to us, "Uncle Lou" if one was formal.

The kid's last name was a bit unusual, so Lou just called him "Eggbeater."

A good leader recognizes talent. Lou recognized some sort of "talent" and recruited him as the water boy. In the days before iced buckets of Gatorade, or hired help to squirt it into the mouths of behemoths, water was carried in a bucket. A galvanized bucket. With a soup ladle. One. All drank from the same ladle. Kids drank from water hoses and shared the same bottle of soda. No one died.

A good leader rewards hard work. Every team needs a mascot. Lou promoted the kid to water boy and mascot. At home games, appropriately attired in shoulder pads, faded jersey, and helmet twice his size, the pint-sized water boy sat on the end of the bench. At the signal he would stumble to the huddle. One hand on the bucket, the other vainly trying to hold the helmet in place, looking through the ear hole. Thirsts sated he'd return to the end of the bench.

The cheerleaders welcomed the mascot into their routines. "Give me an 'A,' Give me an 'M'…"

Well, you know the drill, they'd spell AMITYVILLE! Gee they were pretty! And then the mascot would go sit on the end of the bench. He got to know that end of the bench well. And would in later years as well.

In those days the goal posts were made of wood. When Amityville won, as they usually did, fans would sometimes tear the goal posts down. The coach would be carried off the field on the shoulders of his team. We applauded that. Great leaders deserve that.

Years passed.

It's the fall of '62. Amityville football had amassed a record number of victories over the years.

Good leaders are innovative. Lou would send scouts to watch and film games of teams that we would play in the coming weeks. Armed with this intelligence, he and his assistant coaches would determine the future opponents' best players and the plays they would likely use against us.

Good leaders empower their troops. So it came to pass that a squad of boys was empowered to imitate the teams we would play each week. The squad was formed from the ranks of the smallest team members. The scrawny kid joined other scrawny kids to form what today might be called a "taxi squad." The third stringers. The bench warmers.

Good leaders instill a sense of pride into their troops. Amityville teams are called "Crimson Tide" or "Warriors." That special squad of scrawny kids became mighty warriors… "The Mau Maus!"

A good leader instills spirit. To quote Lou from his book, *The Modern Short Punt*, "The most important factor in winning is not how big you are but how spirited you are!" Teddy Roosevelt claimed "It's not the size of the dog in the fight …it's the size of fight in the dog!" Terriers all, the Mau Maus had plenty of spirit. One might believe that supercharged "spirit quotient" would add 25 pounds of physical muscle to a player. Laws of physics being what they are, we needed 50. Even the fiercest terriers find the going tough when fighting a pack of Rottweilers.

So, every afternoon, we'd display the next team's plays to our teammates. Friends since grade school, but they much bigger and stronger. It was fun, but we'd get trounced.

Great leaders use a bit of psychology against their team's opponents. Those who play the position of "tackle" are generally HUGE guys. The writer from *Newsday* wrote articles prognosticating the coming weeks' games. He brought a photographer to one of our rainy afternoon chalk board sessions. Lou drew some sort of imaginary play onto the blackboard. He called two "tackles" up to the board. They were the scrawny kid and another about the same size. The photographer snapped the picture. It appeared in *Newsday*. The other teams' players saw the tiny "tackles." They figured our team would be pushovers. They would be surprised. They would get hurt. Badly.

Friday before Saturday's game all team members wore white shirts and "V" neck black sweaters. Even the Mau Maus.

Saturday morning we'd all go to church. Although some might be heathen urchins, we all went. Football is not a game for the faint of heart. You try to beat the other guy, mentally and physically. Like boxing. Except we have padding. And helmets. Sometimes even the correct size.

Followed by a breakfast. Hosted by our parents. Served by the cheerleaders. Breaking bread with our friends. We rarely, unfortunately, break bread with our enemies. Maybe we should—someday.

Great leaders have confidence, passion, charisma, and set goals. They want to win. We were asked at the beginning of the season, "Do you want to be on a winning team?" No slackers need apply. If it was a big game, Lou would set up a tape recorder in the locker room. Reel to reel. Playing college football fight songs. Martial music is written and played to motivate. It started the process.

Lou was famous or infamous for his pep talks. There were some who had an issue with that. One had to be there. Plenty of football games have been won in the last seconds of the fourth quarter. Tenacity has stood some of us well under trying circumstances in later life. Never Quit! If you've been there you understand.

The games are a blur. We lost the first two and won the rest. The Mau Maus played in every game. Briefly. Kick offs. Punt returns. Whenever the opposing team's first string, ravaged by our first string, sent in their second, or third. The scrawny kid got to play. A bit. And also saw plenty of time near the end of that bench. We rarely sat. We stood near the sidelines and screamed encouragement to our teammates. Action verbs generally. Best not repeated for delicate ears. Some would be hoarse for days after.

Win or lose, there was always a victory party. Some say there might also have been beer. Hmmm.

June, 1963, graduation, we all moved on, scattered to the four winds.

Lou had a few maxims for us to live by: "Never quit," "DESIRE" (If you want it bad enough you will win!), "Never quit," "Football is a game of inches," "Never quit." Did I say "Never quit?"

Philosophically, football can, in a way, be seen as a metaphor for life. The more spirit you put into it…the more you get out of it.

NEVER QUIT!

Thank you Lou.

"Eggbeater"

MEMORIES

by Kim Ireland

Graduating from eighth grade, the thought of entering high school as a freshman was downright scary. Stories of being "captured" in the woods surrounding the school by upperclassmen to me meant I better find a way to toughen up. And the best way to do that was participate in sports after school.

After making it through freshman year sports, sophomore year was scary as the focus now was playing at varsity level where the hitting in football was serious and if you didn't do it right, it hurt. Fortunately, an enthusiastic coach, Lou Howard, showed us how to be competitive through hard work and long practices. His devotion to creating a cohesive team was an example the whole team related to. He gave it his all, and we as a team followed suit. It was an exciting time as we learned lifelong lessons producing results through dedication to practice and hard work.

Family came first with Lou. He had six kids as I recall and a dedicated wife who ran the household so he could pour his efforts into coaching his football team. We loved the guy and would do all we could for him. Without a doubt his coaching provided the most meaningful lessons in high school.

His friendly intensity was a key to his success. Always in motion, with a coffee nearby.

And super positive about everything he was involved in. A truly great guy I'll always remember.

COACH LOU HOWARD, THE MAN, HIS MISSION AND HIS GIFT

by Brud Yates

The Man: I first met the coach when I was in the eighth grade. I don't remember the details, only that he said he was looking forward to me playing football for Amityville. Back then training meant doing push ups before bed. I could easily do a hundred. I was fired up. The coach had gotten to me. Next time we talked it was the summer before my sophomore year. He called me to come to his house. I remember driving to his house and I really remember the drive home. Coach Howard told me he was bringing me up to play on the varsity. In short, Coach believed in me and from that moment on I believed in me! I trace my confidence back to him. That was the power of the man. He loved his wife Margaret, his children, and he loved coaching football for Amityville High School. His enthusiasm was overwhelming. He was beyond inspirational. He was one of a kind. He was so real. He was the "Man" and I still feel proud that I played for him.

His Mission: Coach Howard lived to win football games for Amityville High School. And win he did. He was a coach's coach. He simply loved the game and it loved him. My teammate at Georgia Tech, Bill Curry, met Coach Howard at a national conference and he has never forgotten him. Coach Howard was like that. He could get your attention and you would never forget him and his love for the game. While Coach Howard won way more games than his share, I think his real mission was to love his life and all of the people in it.

His Gift: Coach Howard's gift to me was his love for coaching. There were times when I was playing for him that I resisted some of his tactics. But over the years I realized that this same resistance inspired me to find my way to express my love for coaching. Playing football in college for Georgia Tech was both the best and hardest thing I've ever done. The hardest parts inspired me to learn how to work hard and follow Coach Howard's lead and make it fun for me and for others. The eastern phrase, "We teach best what we most need to learn" described my challenge. I needed to learn how to settle down, be present and operate more at acceptance. In the process, I could feel myself becoming more like Coach Howard!

Thanks, Coach Howard. The Man you were has made it easier for me to become the man I still want to be. I'm so happy I got to be part of your mission. And most of all, the gift you gave me changed my life.

Reflection: The last time we were together I urged Coach Howard to get me into the Amityville Athletic Hall of Fame. My real motivation was to come back to acknowledge him. As I finished my plea, he remembered a not so good play that I had made that caused us to lose a game. As I pleaded with him to rewrite a nearly 60-year-old performance, the coach was clear. I was supposed to punt and I didn't. While we couldn't recall what I did that wasn't right…he was still my coach. And I loved it!

REMEMBERING LOU HOWARD

by Bruce Chattman

During our lives, we have often seen posts and tweets on social media or heard conversations regarding the "good old days." These anecdotes, memes and reminiscences reflect personal stories, memories of growing up and recall a time when all things are remembered as being less stressful, less regimented, less restricted, and generally happier times. Sometimes, these stories often become the basis of urban legends. Amityville was, and remains, full of many urban legends that are "shrined in our memories where're we may be..." Some of these urban legends were based on facts (rum-running and Al Capone), others derived from events (*The Amityville Horror*) and others were pure fantasy (*Jaws*). But sports is an area where Amityville has had many true legends, none any more than football. Among these are Bernie Wyatt, John Niland and Louis T. Howard, the person who coached and mentored these two outstanding professional athletes as well as many other Amityville athletes and students.

Bernie Wyatt graduated from AMHS in 1957. Bernie was several years older than those of us in the Bailey Homes and grew up just down the street. Because athletics was a focus for us, he was our first personal AMHS football legend. Bernie was an outstanding tailback at Amityville and broke Jim Brown's high school scoring record. He received a scholarship to the University of Iowa where he played in the 1959 Rose Bowl, won the team's MVP in 1960 and was drafted by the Pittsburg Steelers. He went on to coach at the high school and college level in the '70s and ended his career coaching at the University of Wisconsin.

John Niland graduated from AMHS in 1962 and was a classmate, friend, and teammate. John, like Bernie, also attended the University of Iowa on an athletic scholarship where he was a two-time All American. Upon gradation, he was drafted in the first round by the Dallas Cowboys, where he played on the starting line for most of his professional career. During his career, John played in seven consecutive Pro Bowls, two Super Bowls and in 2020, he was selected to the Dallas Cowboys All-Time Team.

Louis T. Howard—"Uncle Lou" as he was affectionately called—is also an urban legend that transcends many generations; a legend based upon fact, influence, impact, and inspiration. In addition to Bernie Wyatt and John Niland, Uncle Lou had a profound influence and impact on many football players, including those who were not on the "First Team." He was a man of faith who was non-judgmental but principled and one who provided structure, tradition, commitment and confidence for all his players; values that they carried with them after they left high school.

I reached out to classmates from my generation, asking for their memories about Uncle Lou and his influence and impact on their lives. Their comments are included here.

Susie Falkenbach Welch wrote:

Uncle Lou! How lucky we were as Amityville students to have had Lou Howard in our lives. For all of my years in Amityville, he was our beloved football coach…beloved for multiple reasons. That he was successful, I guess, would have to be listed first, but his connection with not only his players but also with the other students and the community was extraordinary. For example, my older sister Carol, Class of 1959, wore her fairly short blond hair in a little flip, and, for a while, she dated a classmate who was on the football team. Uncle Lou came up with a nickname for her—"little Dutch girl." He used it always, and I'm sure it made her feel special.

Uncle Lou lived down the street from us on South Bayview Avenue, he was our drivers' education teacher, he was our friend, and he was an icon. Because I still had family in Amityville, I remained somewhat aware of his accomplishments, such as being mayor of Amityville and a state assemblyman, even after I moved away in 1966. Until my 50th class reunion in August 2011, though, I really had no idea of all that he was and all that he did besides what I knew as a student at AMHS. He met with a group of us during that reunion weekend at his little museum in the village. I know most of us were wowed, once again by him, and by the display of memorabilia from his amazing life. He was, that weekend in August 2011, almost 88, but he still seemed young and vibrant.

Once again, Uncle Lou showed this uncanny ability to make those around him feel special, even though it was he who was the special one, not just to us students and football players and the Amityville community, but also to people all over the county, the state, and the country. In a perfect world, every kid would have an Uncle Lou (and an "Aunt Margaret," too, I guess, since she was the one who shared him with all of us).

* * *

Charles Schwarzbeck remembered:
In the autumn of 1960 I was still a shy and unsure member of a family who moved from the city to Amityville, and didn't really fit in. And I was a very small AMHS ninth grader who loved and dreamed about football—especially Amityville football. I dreamed of playing, and I felt embarrassed when I went to try-outs, and tried to begin my "football career." It wasn't even a slight consideration. I still remember that no one told me; I just knew. I walked home, continuing to throw my football in the air and catch it.

A month later I met older cheerleaders who suggested I ride on the fan bus to the first football game. I said "yes," they laughed, and a few days later I was on the bus. Most of the riders were cheerleaders and girls. I sat by myself, in the back, and wondered where I'd go or sit when we arrived.

There was a big crowd. (I don't remember what school we were visiting.) It was the first "big time" football game that I ever attended. I remember that we won, and won again, and again!

The cheerleaders suggested that I lead a cheer from the back of the bus. I yelled "Give me an A...," and the rest of the riders did! We did the A-M-I-T-Y-V-I-L-L-E cheer many times at each game. People would feel something hopeful, and they would turn and look at me. We sang "HooRah for Amityville" when our bus stopped in different villages. I felt proud and less shy.

Yet, when we returned to AMHS, I usually walked home alone. One weekday, late in the football season, I finished running on our track, and I was walking across the fields toward our school. A man's voice called from behind me, "Charlie...Charlie..." I turned around, and there was Lou Howard. He was with Allie Leftenent and John Niland. I didn't know them, and they were happy to see me! Coach Howard told me the players heard us cheer and it was important in getting wins. I remember seeing Allie and John as really strong and impressive. They were nice to me. John said, "Thank you, Charlie". Coach Howard walked next to me and kept his hand on my shoulder.

I could hardly believe it as I walked home. That made me much more than happy. Lou Howard thanked me, and even though I was one of only a few boys on the bus, I thought. I continued leading cheers...And Lou Howard reached out to me and showed me he knew me, I belonged. I was an important contributor. He changed the way I thought about myself: I went on to do and lead what I believed in. I still do. Thanks, Coach!

By 1961 I returned to Brooklyn (where we lived before Amityville), commuting with my mom to Brooklyn Technical H.S. I swam with the Knickerbocker Swim Club.

Even though I was on the first team, it was like swimming in secret. I was back in Brooklyn, but my life was in Amityville. I practiced three nights a week, and we had swim meets in the city on Saturdays.

My AMHS friends played sports at school, and friendships grew out of teams. It was hard for me to make friends.

We had an assembly when I was in the 10th grade, honoring our football, basketball, wrestling, track and baseball teams. It was great, and the varsity players were really pumped up. Lou Howard was there, and he congratulated all of the athletes.

When the assembly ended and the crowd was leaving, I heard a familiar voice call my name. It was Lou Howard. He said, "Charlie....Where have you been...I know where you've been...You've been swimming....I heard you're doing great!" My classmates heard him! He walked with me to my locker. Coach Howard encouraged me to tell him about Brooklyn Tech and the swim club. Several students stayed with us when we talked.

I remember that Coach Howard was excited for me, and that I felt public and proud. Since that day my baseline is open and secure...Lou Howard did that!...And I wondered: How did Coach Howard know about swimming and Brooklyn?

A month later we had a swim meet on a Sunday at the New York Athletic Club. I was a backstroker, and I was practicing flip turns in a "foreign" pool. As I swam laps and flipped, I thought I saw a familiar face in the stands. When I got out of the water my coach was there, and I only saw my mom and dad in the stands. It was crowded and loud.

Then, when my backstroke event was announced, I happened to look up, and there was Lou Howard with his amazing and reassuring smile! He pointed at me, called "Charlie", and he pointed his hand and forefinger straight up, #1. The competition from New York, New Jersey, and Connecticut was tough. I won!

I looked up at my parents, and at Coach Howard. When I came out of the locker room Coach Howard was gone. (I never learned how Lou found out about my swimming, or how he made his way on that Sunday to the N.Y.A.C.) By Wednesday of that week, lots of students knew I was swimming on a city team, and that I won!

I don't know if it was cause-and-effect, but I took a chance and made our HS baseball team, and I tried for student council, and class office and won.

I know that Lou affirmed that I was respected, I was a winner, and I could lead. My 15-year-old shyness and uncertainty were no contest for Lou's assertions.

My comfort with being athletic and with being a leader has been my baseline since then. Two years later he helped me connect with a swim coach at Harvard. I stayed there during spring vacation, and worked out. That led to my going to Kenyon College and swimming there. I remember talking with a college swim coach about Lou Howard. I remember how I realized that I hadn't really gotten to know him. He was supportive of me. He just was. He was such a selfless, smart and helpful friend

I had graduated from Kenyon and Boston University and returned for a visit to Amityville in 1970. Walking down Broadway, I heard this voice, "Hello, Big Guy!" It was Coach Howard!

He bought me a late lunch, and asked me to tell him about my travels from Cambridge, MA, swimming, to college in Ohio, to graduate school in Boston. He asked me what I would do next and I said, "Laboratory science, clinical psychology or medical school."

He sat back with a big smile and he said assuredly, "You don't need to know yet!" I was thinking, "Here I am 24 years old, I'm still mostly training, and I'm broke. And Coach Howard is a great, esteemed football coach. How would he know?" I told him what I thought, and he laughed.

He told me that he had also been at school—in aerospace!—and that he studied aerospace science, and he had just founded the Department of Aerospace in a local college, and that he planned to grow a respected pilot training program. He added, "I don't know what I will do next!"

Here was Lou Howard, again, teaching me how to go with my heart, really make a difference for people, and to patiently make my own path at high levels, and then contribute big with passion.

I got to touch base often with brief telephone check-ins. I called him as I trained and discovered, in Texas, Washington, DC, London, Seattle, and Vancouver. Every time he was warm and energized, and we compared notes on our personal journeys.

Again, Lou Howard coached me and gave me what my mom, dad, and professors couldn't: He showed me how to keep experimenting, to keep learning, to keep creating, and to deliver results that really matter.

In the early 2000s, we talked and I told him how full, confident, and happy I was. I asked him what he was doing. He started telling me about his flying to Europe, and his aviation, and pilot trainer programs. We had to end our call prematurely and we didn't talk again. Lou Howard taught me without being my teacher, supported and encouraged me without being my parent, and he showed me how to run with the ball when I didn't play football. I hope I can be selfless and a great contributor, and a great leader like Lou was. Thanks, Coach!

* * *

Lillian Du-Bois-Shelton reminisced:

He was Uncle Lou to everyone. He was my Drivers' Ed teacher. Whenever you were in his presence you had a smile on your face. He always had a joke to tell. He knew his students. You were family. During those days we had so much racism. But Uncle Lou treated everyone the same. I'm a black woman who truly loved and respected him.

* * *

Steve Leonti recalled:

I grew up around the corner from Uncle Lou's house on S. Bayview Ave. I can remember so many times when we kids rode our bikes by his house and he would always wave to us and ask how we were doing. If he saw us walking to school, he always asked if we wanted a ride. In short, he always looked out for "his kids" in the neighborhood. He was a great man that I know is sadly missed by everyone who was lucky enough to have known him.

* * *

Butch Devine wrote:

Lou Howard was my drivers' education instructor in high school. I remember that we had two girls in the car for driving lessons. In preparation for an emergency, Uncle Lou made the girls change a tire on the car. There was no four-way lug wrench! Just the old single handle type. He told me not to laugh!

At one of the reunions, I asked Uncle Lou to sponsor my dad and me for the Amityville High Hall of Fame in 2013. We were the 1st Father and Son Suffolk County Wrestling Champions. Dad and I were inducted in 2013. After AMHS, I attended the University of Iowa where I was a 3-year starter for the Hawkeyes

You didn't have to play football to be supported and recognized by Uncle Lou. He was respectful of all people!!!

* * *

John Niland recalled:

"Uncle Lou" was always encouraging to me and other players. My dad was an alcoholic and of course, that wasn't really talked about back then. He knew I sometimes had it tough at home. He was so generous with us players and was always opening his home to us. We had meetings there, always fed. His house was like our clubhouse of sorts. Lou always encouraged us, without browbeating, to have a spiritual life; he encouraged us to go to church. He was a shining example to this kid from the wrong side of the tracks.

He was such a class act. Uncle Lou made it a point to stay in touch with the young men he mentored all through their lives and careers. Lou Howard was like a father to me and I am sure there are many others who will say the same thing. He left a positive legacy behind and touched the lives of more young men than he will ever know. "See you in the Kingdom, Coach!"

* * *

Bruce Chattman, my personal story:

My relationship with Coach Howard started early. All of us boys living in the Bailey Homes were interested in playing sports. We were also inspired specifically to play football by the example and recognition earned by Bernie Wyatt, just a few years older than we were and living just a few houses down the street on Bailey Drive. Bernie was a standout running back for AMHS, wore the revered #31 jersey, eclipsed Jim Brown's scoring record for Long Island high schools and earned an athletic scholarship to the University of Iowa. We would watch Bernie play for the Hawkeyes on TV and we all were eager to become part of the AMHS football tradition.

Little League, Cub Scouts, Boy Scouts, church and school sports provided me with many role models and mentors throughout my youth—folks who helped to develop my character and shape my values. But it was when I was at St. Paul's

Lutheran Church and I was about ten years old that I met the man who would significantly and forever impact upon my life—Louis T. Howard.

Sunday School ran concurrent with the Sunday Service and upon exiting my lessons, and waiting for my parents, I often noticed a man surrounded by many post-service congregants engaged in conversations. He had a friendly face, a kind smile and a commanding presence. Intrigued, I asked my Sunday School Teacher who this man was. My Sunday school teacher was Bob Boehm, teenage son of our Pastor. Bob responded, "Why, he is my football coach, Lou Howard." He asked me if I'd like to meet him and after my enthusiastic "Yes," introduced me to Coach Howard. Within a few minutes of meeting and talking with him, I knew then that I definitely was going to play football for this gregarious and charismatic man!

All my friends from the Bailey Homes were one year ahead of me in high school and all of them were good enough to be either on the JV or Varsity team when I was a freshman. Being very competitive, I was motivated to achieve the same status and was successful not only in making the JV team but I also was a starter at tackle. Uncle Lou got to know all of us on the JV Team and would offer words of encouragement and acknowledgement to me when he saw me in the halls or in the locker room. But it wasn't just me and other football players whom he acknowledged. As a drivers' education teacher, he eventually got to know all students and would relate to them, always in a caring and supportive way—often using humor and knowledge based upon his observations and awareness of our successes both in and out of school. He would frequently come up with nicknames for students that reflected something about them he knew was personal and important to them. He would endeavor and succeed in treating everyone as an individual—unique and special. It was this innate ability he had to make everyone feel appreciated that made him such and endearing and motivating coach, mentor and teacher, with relationships lasting lifetimes. For me, personally, Uncle Lou was about to change my life's path, with words of wisdom and advice when I was a junior in high school and again with specific advocacy for me when I was a senior.

I made Varsity as a sophomore and was on the starting line where I played tackle on offense and linebacker on defense. Unfortunately, I broke my leg in the first game and had to spend the rest of the season on the sideline. This, interestingly, provided me with an opportunity to observe and appreciate Lou's intensity for the game and close relationship with the rest of the players on the team, a perspective I would have missed had I been actively playing in the game. Being on Varsity, however, I was also able to attend the Sunday afternoon meetings at Lou's home where we watched films of our Saturday games and were treated as his extended family. It was during these times that Lou got to know me better, including my aspirations for after high school. He learned that because of my family's finances, my only path to college was through an athletic scholarship for either football and/or wrestling (another sport in which I performed well). He also learned of my intense personal interest in attending one of the U.S. Service Academies because my dad was a WWI and WWII Veteran who had served in the Navy.

Colleges would send assistant coaches as recruiters to AMHS to talk to Lou and meet players who they perceived as having potential. During my junior year, representatives from the Ivy League, Big 10 and Big East came specifically to recruit and view game films of our best senior lineman, John Niland. As a junior, I was fortunate to continue my position as a starter and Lou made sure that I was also in these meetings and also pointed me out to them in the game films they reviewed. At 6'2" and 220 lb., I received preliminary interest and attention from the recruiters and Uncle Lou ensured that I was also on their consideration list for "next year's admissions." I was not fortunate to receive guidance and strategies for college admissions from my parents because neither of them nor any members of my extended family had ever attended college. I was the first in my family who had the opportunity to attend college and, because of my academic standing and athletic abilities, I was hopeful of receiving financial aid. There was also neither advice nor practice to pick a "fallback" school or opportunities for "college shopping" such as is the norm in today's society. Consequently, I was very appreciative and dependent upon the encouragement, advice, recognition, support and endorsements that Coach Howard provided for me. Lou was always raising expectations and encouraging everyone to achieve and become all they could be—on and off the field.

My preferred choice for post high school was to attend one of the academies and this desire was enhanced by the appeal that the entire cost of attending them was borne by them in exchange for your commitment to serve as active military, post graduation. My guidance counselor was less than enthusiastic about my interest in the service academies, downplayed my chances of gaining admission and actively tried to discourage me. When I informed Uncle Lou about this, he encouraged me to trust my instincts and to complete the applications for the academies. He further expressed his opinion that I was the type of well-rounded student sought by the academies and based on his encouragement I submitted these applications. In addition, Uncle Lou actively discouraged me from applying just to the big "Football Schools" because of my academic standing, well-rounded experiences, and good SAT scores that would likely result in receiving some financial assistance. His specific words were that I had "too much potential to just rely only on my football abilities" for my future. He told me that I was "more than just a football player" and that I would qualify academically for these schools and for the academies.

During the first half of my senior year, Lou set me up with meetings with coaches Yovicsin, Blackman, and Donelli from Harvard, Dartmouth, and Columbia, respectively. Then after taking my SATs again, I applied to Harvard and Dartmouth because I desired to attend college further away from the urban environment of

NYC (Columbia). My thought process was that these would be my "alternative colleges" should I not receive an appointment to one of the academies. Once all my college applications were submitted, Uncle Lou continuously contacted the schools' football coaches to advocate for me. It was obvious from the regular contact I received from the coaches that they were kept aware of my achievements both on and off the field by Uncle Lou.

Uncle Lou's belief in me, his personal support, efforts, and advocacy on my behalf, resulted in me also receiving invitations to visit and to meet with the coaches from both Annapolis and West Point. Unlike other collegiate institutions, admission to any of the academies is dependent upon nominations by members of Congress. Their communications also informed me how the athletic departments at the academies assisted in applicants receiving these critical congressional appointments and that final admission to either academy was contingent upon the candidate passing both a physical fitness test and a comprehensive medical exam.

In late September, I received a letter from the head football coach inviting me for an October visit to West Point. While there, I met with the team coaches and was escorted around the campus by members of the football team; I observed cadets marching in formation and ate lunch with the plebes—even having to "brace" along with them as we ate. Around the same time in September, I received a formal invitation with two tickets from the head coach at Annapolis inviting me to attend the Army-Navy game as his guest. The invitation was accompanied by a very encouraging letter and set a date for me to visit the Naval Academy in April (contingent upon a Congressional Appointment) where I would meet coaches, take a tour, and receive both my physical and medical exams. I immediately showed both these letters to Uncle Lou and he shared my delight and enthusiasm, offering continuing words of encouragement.

Beyond my highest expectations, I received two letters in early March from

Congressmen. One notified me of my appointment to the U.S. Naval Academy (Annapolis) and the other notified me of my appointment to the U.S. Military Academy (West Point). Included with the letters was information about the ranking hierarchy for both academies compiled by their admissions staff. For the USNA, I was the First Alternate with only one person, the Principal Appointment, ahead of me for admissions. For the USMA, I was the Second Alternate, basically meaning I was third in line for admissions. West Point's letter included a date in March for both physical and medical tests at Fort Dix, NJ, which I subsequently passed. The letter from the USNA indicated that my appointment for the tests would be set only if the principal appointee declined admission.

In late April, I received notification from both Harvard (acceptance) and Dartmouth (waitlisted) regarding my admissions status. Also in April, each of the academies updated me on my admission and appointment status. West Point had moved me to First Alternate and Annapolis confirmed that the Principal Appointee had declined his acceptance and I would be granted admission, class of 1967. Both would be contingent on completion of a fitness test and medical evaluation. Since the Naval Academy was my first choice I was ecstatic and overjoyed.

The first person after my parents with whom I proudly shared all of this wonderful information, especially my acceptances at both Harvard and the Naval Academy, was Uncle Lou. He told me, "You always make me proud. Keep it up." I think he was happier for me than I was for myself.

Knowing of my acceptance at the U.S. Naval Academy and of my next-in-line place at the U.S. Military Academy, I wrote to Harvard admissions and declined my acceptance with a separate letter of appreciation to Head Coach Yovicsin for his support. I also wrote to Dartmouth admissions asking to be removed from their waitlist with a letter of appreciation also sent to Coach Blackman. So, it was a done deal—the United States Naval Academy, here I come! Just the physical and medical exams left to complete!

My visit to the Naval Academy started out to be an exciting day for me. The morning at Annapolis included about three hours devoted to the physical fitness test, which I passed as anticipated. I also had the opportunity to meet with some members of the football team, including Roger Staubach who led Navy to victory at the Army-Navy game that I saw the previous November. The afternoon was a traditional medical exam, including eye and ear testing. I wore glasses/contacts and had already received a "waiver" for the eyesight requirement and passed all the routine tests. The hearing test was the last component for the medical exam. It began with a "whisper" exam, whereupon I was asked to stand in a long (about 20') tunnel-like room with a Petty Officer at the far end. His responsibility was to whisper words to me and my responsibility was to repeat these words. I was distraught to learn that I had failed to respond correctly to his whispers and was referred to a Navy Audiologist, who performed a complete hearing evaluation including an audiogram. Upon completion of this evaluation, I was informed that I had a substantial hearing loss and this would most likely prevent me from passing the medical exam and jeopardizing attending Annapolis. It was a very long ride home.

Having withdrawn my applications to both Harvard and Dartmouth, my lone remaining option for a college education was relegated to the person ahead of me in the admission line for West Point. In early May, I was notified that he had accepted admission. Here it was May and I was out of options. Despondent, I had a long, heartfelt discussion with my parents about my future. Enlisting was an option that I was prone to take, especially considering the possibility of benefits such as the GI Bill, career training, etc. My Dad, a veteran of two world wars, was very discouraging of this option. Having had a perfunctory, disappointing experience with my guidance counselor, the family decision was for me to seek advice and counsel from Uncle Lou.

Uncle Lou was intimately involved with my early interactions with Columbia, Harvard, and Dartmouth coaches and he knew that I had not applied to Columbia. I had kept him informed of all my positive progress with both of the academies and he knew of my excitement and hopes to attend one of the academies were paramount in my heart and mind. He also knew of my acceptance at Harvard and being waitlisted at Dartmouth. Because of this excitement and progress with the academies, however, I neglected to inform him that I sent a non-acceptance letter to Harvard and took myself off the waitlist for Dartmouth. When I went to Uncle Lou to inform him of the dire situation I created by my decisions to do these things, he was not the least bit pleased with me. He communicated his displeasure to me with a coach's voice and mode as clearly as if he was screaming at me and pounding on my helmet for a missed block, bad tackle, or getting a penalty flag.

However, once he was done being my coach, the "Uncle" in him took over and he was extremely empathetic, kind, and supportive. We discussed options available to me that I had not pursued or considered. Although it was late May and colleges had already made their admission decisions, Lou knew something I didn't; that there was always room created by accepted students who chose not to attend, who did not report, students who dropped out, health issues, etc. He also knew that people could be added to the waitlist, even jump to the front of the list if the college had specific needs to fill. We talked about local Long Island colleges like Hofstra, Adelphi, C.W. Post (LIU) and others but he suggested and encouraged me to pursue admission to Columbia because of the early interest they had expressed in me. While it was too late in the process to request financial aid and I was concerned about costs, Lou urged me to pursue admission and worry about paying for it later. He offered to call the Columbia coaching staff about me and to ask what could be done. Uncle Lou made the call and they were very responsive and helpful and

initiated contact with the Admissions Office on my behalf.

After a few subsequent conversations with the admissions staff, Uncle Lou and I were cleared to make a final direct call to the Director of Admissions, Dean Coleman, so I could explain my situation and plead my case. After a conversation of only about 15 minutes, Dean Coleman told me, "If you have the grades, SAT scores and meet all of Columbia's other standards, we would make room for you." I had the AMHS school office send him all the required information and within a week, I received a phone call for an appointment to meet face-to-face with Dean Coleman. After my meeting with Dean Coleman, I was informed by him that I would be admitted and subsequently received a formal letter of admission for the Columbia Class of 1967.

Uncle Lou's advocacy, assistance, and encouragement saved my future. As things evolved, I had a wonderful and enlightening collegiate experience resulting in lifelong friendships, a great and productive career with a resulting successful and meaningful life because of my opportunity to attend Columbia. None of this would have happened had it not been for the support and encouragement I consistently received from Uncle Lou.

In 2012, I last saw and spoke with Lou in person at the 50th Reunion for the AMHS Classes of '62 and '63. He was in attendance with his lovely wife, Margaret, as they were our guests of honor. Uncle Lou put his arm around me, gave me a squeeze and said, "You always made me proud, keep it up." At age 88, he was still my mentor, encouraging me and gently setting expectations.

Thank you, Uncle Lou. You made a difference in my life and the lives of hundreds of others.